How you can do more in less time

How you can do more in less time

Clive T. Goodworth

Business Books

London   Melbourne   Sydney   Auckland   Johannesburg

Business Books Ltd

An imprint of the Hutchinson Publishing Group

17–21 Conway Street, London W1P 6JD

Hutchinson Publishing Group (Australia) Pty Ltd
PO Box 496, 16–22 Church Street, Hawthorn, Melbourne, Victoria 3122

PO Box 151, Broadway, New South Wales 2007

Hutchinson Group (NZ) Ltd
32–34 View Road, PO Box 40–086, Glenfield, Auckland 10

Hutchinson Group (SA) (Pty) Ltd
PO Box 337, Bergvlei 2012, South Africa

First published 1984

© Clive T. Goodworth, 1984

Set in Palatino by Folio Photosetting, Bristol

Printed and bound in England by
Anchor Brendon Ltd, Tiptree, Essex

British Library Cataloguing in Publication Data
Goodworth, Clive T.
   How you can do more in less time.
   1. Executives–Time management
   I. Title
   658.4'093   HF5500.2

ISBN 0 09 159050 7

Dedicated to Paul, Mark, Carl and Anna-Jane – who, although up to their necks in the rat-race, always find time for their Dad.

Contents

1   Time and tide . . .   **11**

The manager and this thing called Time – the
components of 'life room' – a jolting reminder of
vital time wasted – an exercise to bring the point
home – memory-prodder

2   Once upon a time . . .   **27**

An account of John's day at work – a look at his
'actual work', 'work-related obligations' and 'leisure
at work' – the cost of work – a salutary exercise –
memory-prodder

3   A stiff dose of self-management   **43**

The elusive quality of self-discipline – a methodical
approach to the daily grind – organizing time and
effort – some home truths on the basic 'functions
of management' – a self-appraisal exercise –
memory-prodder

4   So what d'you do there, anyway?   **57**

Some managers' innermost thoughts on their work
– an introduction to routine activities, people
activities, thinking and problem-solving – a
selection of nasty attitudes of mind – an exercise in
thinking – memory-prodder

5   Organizing and timing the bread-and-butter stuff   **67**

Coping with the written word – the paperwork empire – surviving the 'information explosion' – an exercise and memory-prodder on relevant skills

6   Organizing and timing the people bit   **79**

A crafty lead-in to a chunk on delegation – giving instructions and passing information – the neglected art of counselling – handling meetings – an exercise in delegation – memory-prodder

7   Come to think of it . . .   **93**

Something to get you thinking – the components of thought: gut-feelings; education and experience; comprehension – a kick-starter for regular and profitable thinking – an exercise in organized thought – memory-prodder

8   Hold on, there's a wee problem   **105**

The manager as a problem-solving machine – the six difficult steps in problem solving – passing the buck – an exercise in timing the solution of a problem – memory-prodder

9   Catching spanners before they get in the works   **115**

A homily on the 'ever-open door' – reducing those wretched interruptions – nasty habits with the telephone – working hours and relaxation – an exercise in the practical audit of your secretary's skills – memory-prodder

10   Getting the act together   **129**

A reminder of the March of Time – Doug Rearden and his attempt to organize time, leading up to an exercise in setting priorities and compiling a work-schedule – a long hard look at time-wasters

11   Miles and miles of time   149

Travelling time: to work or not to work, that is the question – a bit on airborne labours – the travelling businessman's work-kit – planning work on the move – a postscript on travel sickness

12   It'll all come out in the wash   163

Yer better-than-average manager's typical day – being a fly's-eye view of Don Street, and how he achieves his state of management grace – a short, sharp 'adieu'

Recommended reading list   181

Index   182

1 Time and tide . . .

In theory one is aware that the earth revolves, but in pratice one does not perceive it, the ground upon which one treads seems not to move, and one can live undisturbed. So it is with Time in one's Life.

Marcel Proust,
Remembrance of Things Past: Swann's Way

If you are silly enough to make the same mistake as I did, and ask a superbly qualified egg-head for a precise definition of 'time', it's on the cards that he'll come up with something like this: 'Ah, yes, I'm glad you asked me that question. Well, the base unit of the measurable quantity known as time is, of course, the second – and a second is defined as the duration of 9,192,631,770 periods of the radiation corresponding to the transition between the two hyperfine levels of the ground state of the caesium-133 atom. Anything else?

Hmm, I think we'll start again. What, for goodness sake, is this thing we call 'time'? By way of an ice-breaker, let's ponder the question, and, I hope, see in a jiffy that, depending on our point of view, it can have umpteen, very different meanings. For instance, to the pimply adolescent, seething with impatience to quit the nest, time could well be the penal servitude of being hammered from dawn to dusk by parental carping and constraint. Or, if you like, to spindle-legged Miss Plain-Jane, yearning for the love of her life, it could be nothing but the infinitely long road along which she plods in search of romance. There again, to poor old Arthur, aged ninety-three and saddled with a body crying out for respite, time could be reduced to pure physical torture – an interminable suffering that denies him the peace of oblivion. And, of course, to the cold realists in our midst, those who recognize that clocks and calendars are man-made toys, time could be merely a measurement in space – with the earthly hour representing an arc of fifteen degrees in the apparent daily rotation of the celestial sphere.

All right, but what of the manager? What does time mean to the Jacks and Jills of the executive world? Y'know, we could eavesdrop and find out:

'Time is what I've never got – and, judging by the way things are going, never will have . . .'
Wry comment by a young production manager addressing students on an Institution of Industrial Managers' course.

'Time, you say? I tell you what, you should really be asking my boss that question, not me . . . You see, he actually believes there are forty-eight hours in a day! Unfortunately, he only pays me for eight of 'em . . . .'

'I know what my MD'd say if he was here –"Never forget, laddie, time is money"! He may be right – but I wish he'd stop making it an excuse for his constant chivvying . . .'
Observations by manager-students on the same course.

'Whenever talk at work gets round to the question of time – well, that's when I start to worry. More often than not, it's a sure sign that somebody is planning to foist another job on to me. In fact, it's the standard drill, isn't it – first, convince some poor overworked guy that it's always possible to squeeze extra minutes from the day, and then clobber him with a task that'll take ten times as long to even scratch the surface. Why, I reckon there are more bucks passed that way than any other . . .'
Emphatic cry from the heart by a transport manager during a seminar on the management of time.

'Time kills . . .'
A much-favoured comment by an old boss of mine.

Just suppose, if Mother Nature ever did get round to creating an elephants' graveyard for managers (now there's a nice thought), I'm sure the Chapel of Rest would be adorned with a single, solemn epitaph – 'Time is the Enemy'. Unfortunately, the message is loud and clear; far too many managers are engaged in a wholly unavailing, to-the-death struggle with time. It may be all fine and dandy for the astronomer to peek at some star thirty-eight light years away in space and, actually seeing it as it was in 1948, know that he is recalling time – but here's the rub, it doesn't work like that for you and me. Whether we like it or not, we are well and truly stuck with this particular enemy. All we can hope to do is learn how best to live with the speeding horror and, by resort to our native cunning, so organize our activities that we contrive to wring the utmost benefit from each minute of the working day.

And, come to think of it, that is precisely what this book is all about – so, hello and welcome, and let's get cracking!

They call it 'life room'

Whoops, only a couple of paragraphs into the thing and I'm tossing jargon at you – but bear with me, for the term 'life room' is of considerable importance in this preliminary look at Old Father Time's box of tricks. It is a very apt name for the personal aggregate of activities in which you and I engage throughout the span of our existence on this planet; and, as you may feel inclined to believe, when the Great Chairman in the Sky has each of us in for the Last Appraisal, boy, do the contents of those life rooms give the game away . . . But enough of that; the obvious fact is that our highly individual and wide-ranging activities can be, and usually are, conveniently classified as either *work* or jolly old *leisure*. However, to leave it at that would make me guilty of gross over-simplification – so, prith'ee, take a closer look:

'Work'

Since most of us didn't have the luck to be born with a silver spoon for a dummy, we tend to attach but one meaning to the word 'work': quite simply, the daily grind –the paid employment from which we derive, some more successfully than others, the means to live. But there are other forms of activity which, because they cannot be readily classified as 'leisure', must also be grouped under this heading. They include:

Things we do to comply with the rules of our community
- Visit the Post Office to purchase a TV licence.
- Obey a court summons.
- Follow a road traffic diversion.
- If we're British, form a queue.
  etc., etc.

Things we do which are not strictly work, but 'work-related'
- Procure and maintain working garb which we would never dream of acquiring were it not for our employment?
- Commute to and from work.
- Engage in 'obligatory' social discourse with seniors, peers and juniors at work.
- Have the boss and his wife to dinner?
  etc., etc.

'Leisure'

Yes, you've guessed it, the generic term 'leisure' also has a variety of meanings. Firstly, there is the obvious and multivarious bunch of activities which, in sum, comprises doing one's own, obligation-free thing – be it choosing to contemplate one's navel, go for a liver-mincing jog, or go to the local on a Friday night. But then there are the less obvious activities, such as:

Things we do which are 'leisure-related' but obligatory
- Tend the garden although, in truth, we cordially detest the wretched chore.
- Carry out those odd jobs in the home, notwithstanding that we dislike all forms of DIY.
- Talk politely to that infernal bore of a neighbour.
  etc., etc.

Things we do to satisfy our physiological and other 'existence needs'
- Hopefully, sleep the sleep of the just.
- Eat, drink and (again, hopefully) eliminate.
- Wash and groom our beautiful selves.
  etc., etc.

So there we have it, a potted version of life room defined in terms of passing our allotted span in the performance of an infinitely wide range of activities – or, in other words, an expression of the *dimensions* of our earthly existence. It is now necessary for us to zoom-in on that chunk of life room which, for want of unlimited lolly, is devoted by most mortals to the hairy old business of working for a living. In particular, we must examine how Mr (or Ms) Average-Manager tends to regard the dimension of time in relation to work. As a first example, I would like to introduce you to a true-life friend of mine . . .

Brian's life room – the employment bit

Brian is a very able college lecturer who, in addition to his actual teaching commitments, is responsible to his head of department for the overall administration and direction of several management-type courses. Not so long ago, I asked him to assist me in the preparatory work for this chapter by letting me have a detailed list of his activities at work – adding that I wasn't interested in any order of priority or, indeed, the proportion of time he expended on each task. Once he had stopped cursing, he very kindly came up with the following:

1 Preparing notes, etc. for lecture sessions.
2 Compiling course hand-outs.
3 Producing OHP transparencies and other aids.
4 Writing case studies, role plays, etc.
5 Setting examination papers and progress tests.
6 Lecturing to students and other class contact.
7 Marking written work.
8 Conducting tutorials and other student interviews.
9 Maintaining student and other work records.
10 Writing student reports.
11 Discussing work with head of department and colleagues.
12 Attending college committees and other meetings.
13 Curriculum development.
14 Visiting local employers, etc.
15 Liaising with course and other institutions.
16 Compiling memos, returns, etc.
17 Ordering books and other materials.
18 Student enrolment administration.
19 Designing course brochures and other PR material.
20 Private study – keeping up to date in subject areas.

You may feel inclined to agree that Brian's stab at providing me with a list of his activities at work is pretty comprehensive – but, you know, for all that, the information he has supplied is far from complete. The following diagram indicates that one's 'employment life room' comprises three important activity groups and highlights my friend's omissions:

Brian's employment life room

Actual work	←	Work-related obligations	→	Leisure at work
Detailed in his list		Omitted		Omitted

We will be returning to the vexed questions of 'actual work', 'work-related obligations' and 'leisure at work' in some detail later on – so, for the present, suffice it to say that, if Brian wishes to do something about managing his time at work with any degree of effect, he must pay a whole heap of attention to the entire spectrum of his employment life room. And, ramming the point home, *so must we all*.

Bearing in mind that this opening chapter is merely intended as a kind of *hors d'oeuvres* (yes, I know – with this for starters, who needs a main course!), providing some preliminary illustrations of manager types and their attitudes to time, let me draw your attention to an age-old but eminently relevant caveat:

'Sed fugit interea, fugit inreparabile tempus'

or, just in case your Latin is like mine:

'Meanwhile time is flying, flying never to return'

It is a sad fact that many of us tend to flout and ignore time, even when eagle-eyed attention to the passage of minutes and seconds is a vital prerequisite of the job itself. No one in their right mind would deny that today's airline pilot is, among other things, a manager in every sense of the word – a hand-picked, highly trained executive whose very function, to say nothing of the lives of his passengers, depends on his ability to perform within, and adhere to, an exacting, to-the-second timetable of events. Therefore, I make no apology for introducing as my second example of the misuse of time an account which tells of airline pilots – and of a crisis that, far from bringing only frustration and disappointment in its wake, resulted in stark tragedy.

Seventy minutes to live

Those whose job it is to publicize air travel may perhaps be forgiven for constantly reminding Joe Public that flying is a jolly sight safer than crossing the road – for, with no trouble at all, they can produce a heap of excellently impressive figures to prove their point. One such statistic reminds us that, of all the millions of passengers who chose to travel by non-communist airlines in 1978, only 962 were killed in air crashes. This must be comforting – unless, of course, someone *you* knew suffered the dire misfortune of being included within the fatalities, when the statement becomes nothing but a cruel mockery. As I have intimated, this is a description of seventy minutes in the passage of time – and of how, as a result of the misuse of those minutes, eight of those 962 fated souls met their untimely and violent ends.

Even to the most nervous of passengers, there must be something faintly reassuring about the air of utter 'normality' encountered and engendered within the cabin of a jet-age airliner. There is no reason to suppose that the flight attendants aboard United Airlines Flight 173, outward bound from Denver, Colorado on 28 December 1978, did anything but foster and maintain such an ambience for the benefit of the 181 passengers in their care. When the McDonnell Douglas DC8 took off, it was carrying no less than 46,700 pounds of aviation kerosene in its fuel tanks, which should have been more than sufficient for the scheduled two-and-a-half-hour flight to Portland, Oregon. As events turned out, it wasn't. Flight 173 was due to land at Portland at precisely 17.15 hours, but seventy wasted minutes ensured that it didn't – not then or at any other time. What follows is a catalogue of this prelude to disaster:

Hrs.	Mins.	Secs.	
17	05	00	Being well-established on his preliminary descent, the DC8 captain called Portland and informed the approach controller that he was at 10,000 feet and reducing his airspeed. He was cleared for a visual approach to the runway in use and, within minutes, the aircraft's undercarriage and flaps were lowered in preparation for a straightforward landing.
			Suddenly, all was not well. Alerted by a loud noise that resounded throughout the DC8's airframe, the flight crew saw that the cockpit warning lights were indicating an undercarriage malfunction – only the nosewheel had lowered satisfactorily.
			Not surprisingly, the pilot reported the problem and, as a result, the aircraft was instructed to circle at 5,000 feet until the difficulty had been sorted out. The crew did all they could to pinpoint the malfunction but without success.
17	28	00	At about this time the captain radioed United Airlines and informed the company of his predicament. He stated that he had 7,000 pounds of fuel left in his tanks and intended to remain airborne for a further fifteen to twenty minutes to enable the cabin crew to prepare the passengers for an

emergency evacuation on landing. The DC8 continued to circle.

17	46	52	The aircraft's flight engineer reported that the fuel was down to 5,000 pounds, sufficient for approximately twenty-four minutes of flight.
17	49	00	Operating as designed, the cockpit fuel warning lights came on, indicating that the DC8 was low on fuel. The flight crew continued to occupy themselves trying to diagnose the undercarriage malfunction.
17	50	00	The captain told the crew that he intended to land the aircraft in fifteen minutes' time, but the flight engineer questioned the decision, stating that such a delay would reduce the fuel to a dangerously low level. The captain responded by instructing the flight engineer to radio United Airlines at Portland and tell them that he would land the aircraft with 4,000 pounds of fuel on board.
17	55	00	The flight crew completed the approach descent checks.
17	56 (approx)	55	With the remaining fuel down to 4,000 pounds, the captain still did not seem inclined to carry out the landing. Surprisingly, he sent the flight engineer to check on the state of affairs in the passenger cabin.
18	02	10	According to the cockpit voice recorder, at this time the captain was calmly discussing the passengers' state of morale with the flight enginer.
18	02	22	The flight engineer, doubtless now thoroughly alarmed, reported that the fuel was down to 3,000 pounds.
18	03 (approx)	25	Portland air traffic control queried when the DC8 would commence its landing. The captain replied by stating that the cabin crew had just about completed their preparations, and that the landing would take place in 'another three, four, five minutes'. At this point, the aircraft was eight miles away from Portland, *but heading away from the airfield*. The captain once again chose to discuss the undercarriage fault with his now anxious crew.

18	06	19	One of the stewardesses visited the cockpit and stated that the cabin crew were ready for the emergency landing. *At this point, the DC 8 was seventeen miles from Portland.*
18	06	40	The captain announced that he was going to commence his appproach, and that the aircraft should be landing in about five minutes. *One of the DC8's four engines stopped.* This appeared to surprise the captain and he twice queried the reason – to be informed in succinct terms by the first officer that it had run out of fuel. Confusion now reigned on the flight deck.
18	07	02	The captain radioed Portland and requested an immediate clearance for landing, which was granted. *The DC8, now flying on three engines, had nineteen miles to go.* The flight engineer reported that a second engine stoppage was imminent and, after some discussion, convinced the captain that the fuel was well-nigh exhausted. *At this point, the problem was simply one of keeping the DC8 airborne until, frantically changing course, they reached the airfield.*
18	08	45	This is what the cockpit voice recorder revealed: FIRST OFFICER 'Get this *** on the ground.' FLIGHT ENGINEER 'There's not much more fuel.'
18	13	21	*The second engine stopped.* CAPTAIN 'They're all going – we can't make Troutdale.' (Troutdale is a small airfield near Portland) FIRST OFFICER 'We can't make anything . . .'
18	13	36	The captain ordered the first officer to broadcast a 'Mayday', which he did, adding the desperate words 'The engines are flaming out, we're not going to make the airport.'
18	15	00	*Flight 173 crash-landed six miles short of Portland.* Incredibly, 'only' eight passengers, a cabin attendant and the flight engineer were killed, with twenty-one passengers and two crew members sustaining serious injuries.

Reader, you may feel that, in using the tragic example of Flight 173 to highlight man's propensity for ignoring the passage of time, I've been guilty of over-dramatizing the point. Be that as it may, but if it helps to make the message stick, why, all well and good. Virgil had it right:

'Meanwhile time is flying, flying never to return'

And now, since I am a firm believer in spreading the load, it's your turn to do some work!

Self-tutorial

Exercise 1

'Waste time? Not me, boyo – I'm too blinkin' busy!'

Read the following description of Tom Bosworth's day at the office with your usual care. Tom is sales manager at Northbury Hoggs Limited, an old-established and highly reputable company supplying specialist diagnostic and surgical equipment to the medical profession. Having read the account, arm yourself with a pencil and paper and make copious notes on all the occasions when you reckon Tom, whether by negligence or design, managed to waste time. Keep the notes handy, you will need them later on.

Tom arrived at his office to find Anne, his secretary, already at her desk. Fortified by the cup of coffee that always marked the start of the working day, he settled himself at his desk, lit his first pipe of the morning and commenced work on the several bits and bobs in his in-tray. Shortly after nine o'clock, on hearing the faint hum of conversation from the open-plan sales office next door, he rose from his seat and went to check that everyone was present and correct. Noting that two of his sales clerks were still off sick, he was about to query the distribution of work with Mary, the office supervisor, when she smilingly announced that she'd already carried out a reshuffle and thus catered for the absentees. Tom, who was acutely aware that the monthly returns had to be completed and away before the day's end, told Mary that he would see if Accounts could spare a clerk to help out. He straight away phoned Arthur Green, the accountant, who agreed – albeit somewhat grudgingly – to lend the sales department a body for the day. Then, after a few more words with

Mary, he returned to his office.

Once he had resumed his seat, Tom completed the outstanding work from the previous day and started on his next task, correcting the typed draft of his monthly sales report to the managing director. He was working on the report when Anne came in with the morning's mail and, as was her usual practice, discussed with him the initial disposal of the various pieces of correspondence. They had only just finished this when there was a tap at the door and John Napper, the production manager, asked if Tom could spare a moment to help out with some queries concerning a one-off order that had come through the previous day. Anne, who had more than enough work to keep her going, was only too pleased to leave the two men to their discussion. As it happened, Napper's queries were swiftly resolved, but he had no sooner left the room when one of Tom's clerks, Bill Dyer, appeared in the doorway. Apologizing for the interruption, the middle-aged employee said that he had a bit of a problem that he'd like to talk over with Tom, but, if it was inconvenient, he could always come back later in the day. Stealing a glance at his watch, Tom waved Dyer to a chair and told him to take his time over explaining what was wrong. It turned out that Dyer's wife, who suffered badly with arthritis, was becoming increasingly incapacitated and the man was worried that the need to help her first thing in the morning was making it difficult for him to get to work on time. As it happened, Tom had always regarded Dyer as the near-epitome of a perfect employee and hastened to assure him that he was not to worry about arriving a bit late at the office, adding that Dyer had never hesitated to put in more than his fair share of effort and that, as his boss, Tom was fully confident that such loyalty would continue unabated. Dyer expressed his gratitude and, after some further discussion, returned next door, plainly relieved that his problem had been so swiftly resolved.

Tom then resumed work on the draft sales report, and was half-way through the final page when the telephone rang. It was Peter, his son, a newly qualified third officer in the Merchant Navy – and Tom was delighted to hear that the lad, whose ship had just docked at Liverpool, intended to come home for a few days' snatched leave. They talked for a minute or two, and then – promising to meet his son off the train at six that evening – Tom rang off and, smiling to himself, got on with the report. It was just on 10.30 when he finished amending the document to his complete satisfaction and passed it to Anne for re-typing – she promptly reminded him that he was due to attend the bi-monthly management meeting at eleven o'clock. Mindful of the fact that three items on the agenda concerned his department, Tom spent the next half-hour studying the minutes of the last meeting and preparing his arguments for what he knew would be a fairly difficult session. Then, with a final word to Anne, he set off for the conference room.

The meeting, having got off to its accustomed late start, lasted for about eighty minutes, during which time Tom – as he had anticipated – encountered weighty opposition to his proposals. However, his arguments won the day and it was with a slightly jaunty step that he finally returned to his desk, highly satisfied with the way things had gone. Anne had taken good advantage of his absence to type a number of letters for his signature and, having completed this small chore, Tom proceeded to make his customary round of the department – checking this and that, speaking to those of his sales representatives who happened to be in at the time and paying particular attention to the progress of the two girls who were responsible for tele-sales. Then, content that everything was ticking over smoothly, he returned to his own office – where he found Jim Stanton, the company's PR consultant, who had arrived early for his weekly appointment and was enjoying a cup of coffee while chatting to Anne.

The two men knew each other well and wasted no time in getting down to business. As was their wont, at about one o'clock they adjourned to a nearby pub where they continued to talk shop over a ploughman's lunch. At one stage in the informal session, Stanton produced from his briefcase the preliminary artwork of a new brochure for Tom's inspection and approval and, typical of his breed, was a trifle put out when the sales manager gave it a less than enthusiastic reception. They discussed the project at some length and, still not convinced that the artwork was suitable, Tom undertook to seek the views of his representatives – who were all due at the office at 2.30 for the weekly sales get-together. He promised that he would telephone Stanton later in the afternoon with a final verdict – and, at that, the two men drained their glasses and, after a few more words, left the pub and went their separate ways.

On his return to the office, Tom found that his wife had telephoned, leaving a request that he should ring her back at the earliest opportunity. Wondering what had happened, he made the call and learned from his wife that their young daughter had been sent home from school with all the symptoms of Asian 'flu. The

22

doctor had been in to see her and had prescribed some medicine but, since Tom had the car, it would be necessary for him to collect the prescription on his way home from work that evening – or earlier, if he could manage it. Tom said he would do his best but, because of the sales meeting, for which he was already late, he might not be able to get the medicine until his normal coming-home time. Tom then said a hasty goodbye to his better half and, looking anxiously at his watch, strode rapidly to the conference room.

Having apologized to the assembled representatives for his tardy appearance, Tom plunged into the informal agenda for the meeting and the next two hours passed swiftly in animated and occasionally heated debate. The artwork for the new brochure received unanimous disapproval, and this topic alone stimulated much comment from the publicity-minded salesmen. However, the main subject of discussion was the very real fear by all of the representatives that the draconian cuts in national Health Service expenditure would adversely affect their jobs – and Tom was hard pressed to convince all present that the company, mindful of the likely burgeoning of the private medical sector, had no intention to reduce its sales force. He reminded his team that, despite the continuing financial pressure on the NHS, sales over the past six months had actually increased – and, in an effort to further bolster the men's confidence, announced that improved rates of commission would shortly be introduced. The representatives were clearly encouraged by this news and the meeting broke up on a distinctly cheerful note, with much light-hearted banter in evidence as the men jostled through the building on their way out.

Back in his office, Tom found that Anne had re-typed the monthly sales report and he spent a few minutes swiftly checking and signing this, together with a number of other letters which she had produced during his absence. Then, glancing hastily at his watch, he made a number of telephone calls, including one to Jim Stanton concerning the rejected artwork. It was shortly after five o'clock when, his calls completed, Tom began work on the analysis of sales publicity costs over the previous six-month period. As he was reviewing the figures, Mary, the sales office supervisor, tapped on the door and, flourishing a batch of documents, informed him that all the monthly returns had been compiled, adding that, if he could sign them straight away, she would be able to distribute them to the various recipients before she went home that evening. Tom, who prided himself on his department's ability to meet administrative deadlines, was only too pleased to do as Mary requested, and taking the weighty bunch of papers from her, quickly went through them, checking and signing as necessary. This took about eight minutes and it was approaching 5.30 when Tom, having thanked Mary for organizing what had obviously been a splendid team effort, returned to the analysis of publicity costs. He had barely lifted his pen when the telephone rang. It was Martin Brent, the managing director – something had come up, could Tom pop along to see him? The summons was not to be denied and, having said he'd come immediately, Tom left his office – pausing on the way to have a quick word with Anne, who was clearing her desk in readiness for her departure after a busy day's work. On entering Brent's opulently furnished sanctuary, he saw at once from the look on the MD's face that something was wrong and, heaving a mental sigh, resigned himself to the probability that another late session was in the offing. Waving Tom to a chair, Brent wasted no time on his usual preliminary chit-chat, but, instead, announced in an uncharacteristically terse fashion that the company had a crisis on its hands. Tom, who had already suffered one precipitately sudden redundancy in his career, felt his stomach muscles tighten as he waited in silence for the MD to continue. His fears were not assuaged when Brent went on to tell him that the Gifford Group, their parent company, had sold out Northbury Hoggs, lock, stock and barrel, to a US multi-national, the Dakota Surgical Corporation. This, so far as Brent was concerned, could only mean one thing – an almost certain injection of American influence into Northbury Hogg's close-knit management team. He stated that it was far too early to even hazard a guess as to what, if any, changes would be made by the new owners, but that they would probably learn more about this following the first visit by a team from Dakota Surgical in a week's time. Meanwhile, Brent concluded, Tom was to concentrate all his efforts on preparing for what would certainly turn out to be a stringent inspection of the company in general, and the sales department in particular. And that was that.

Tom returned to his office with his head in a whirl, literally staggered by the sudden and intensely worrying turn of events. Scarcely conscious of what he was doing, he wandered aimlessly through the now deserted sales office, eyeing wall-charts without actually seeing them, picking up odd papers without thought for their contents and exhibiting all the classic signs of that sad phenomenon, an executive in shock. It was approaching 6.30 when, suddenly remembering his promise to collect his daughter's

24

prescription, he donned his hat and coat and, still bemused, walked slowly downstairs to his car. The fact that he had completely forgotten to meet his son at the station never entered his head.

Once you have finished shedding tears for Tom's sad lot, please do not forget to put your notes (yes, of course you've made them) safely aside. As I said at the beginning, you'll need them later on.

Memory-prodder 1

You will find that the tail-piece to each chapter consists of one of these little beasts – and, needless to say, you are on your honour to make use of them. Since we've only just started, you are getting away almost scot-free with this first one – but, for all that, get prodding!

a   What exactly is meant by the term 'life room'?
b   What are the three basic components of the 'employment portion' of one's life room?
c   And, just for the hell of it, what exactly is your conception of 'time'?

2 Once upon a time . . .

So conscious he how short time was
For all he planned to do within it
He did nothing at all, alas
Save note the hour – and file the minute
                    Sir Francis Meynell,
                    For a Functionary

. . . there was a manager named John. He was a very average, run-of-the-mill guy who had clawed his way up the promotion ladder to the post of administration manager at, shall we say, the Excelsior Snug-Fit Truss Company. The need to work for a living was indelibly stamped on John's life room and, apart from an occasional pipe-dream of coming up on the Treble Chance, he gave little or no thought to the fact that one-third of his effective adult existence was being expended in the service of others. Mind you, that is not to say that John was an unthinking serf at heart – but, rather, that the business of holding down a job had become, so far as he was concerned, an inescapable fact of life. Being a responsible kind of chap, he firmly believed in giving a fair day's work for a fair day's pay and would have strongly refuted any suggestion that he spent his employer's time in this or that 'non-productive' or 'leisure' activity. In short, he was a man who detested 'skiving' and anyone who indulged in it. Okay, then – so that's John. Since we have to study 'time spent at work' in pretty close detail, I suggest we take up the slide bearing a sample-slice of his employment life room – and plonk it under the microscope.

John's day at work – it's all a matter of time

Concentrate, if you will, reader, on the 'clock' and John's activities in the account of his day which follows. We'll deal with the 'minutes spent' chunk later on.

Clock	Activity	Minutes spent in:		
		Actual work	Work-related obligations	Leisure at work
08.32	As usual, John arrives early at the office. His oft-quoted explanation for this laudable practice is that he likes to 'get in some solid work' before the telephone starts ringing.			
08.32 – 08.37	He visits the loo and what-not, and then settles at his desk.	–	1	4
08.37 – 08.54	He works on various papers in his in-tray, one of which triggers him to think about a certain difficult colleague, and the prospect that the man could cause him some trouble. Being only human after all, his mind flicks back to home and the breakfast conversation with his wife – bills, bills and more bills . . .	14	–	3
08.54 – 09.02	Mary, his secretary, arrives. Being a decent boss, John opens the official day by chatting amiably with her about this and that – and the conversation gradually gets round to work topics.	5	3	–
09.02 – 09.11	Mary departs to make the coffee, and John gets to grips with yesterday's outstanding work. He is interrupted by Mary, who brings in his coffee and the morning post – and, a moment later, by the entrance of Bill, the firm's accountant, who habitually drops by for a pow-wow (and a free coffee) around this time.	8	½	½
09.11 – 09.20	Under the guise of talking shop, the two men discuss the MD's			

unexpected outburst at the last management meeting and, more to the point, the probable domestic tiff that provoked his ill-humour. They also talk about the planned office extension and how, despite their combined opposition to the scheme, the board of directors seem determined to commit financial hara-kiri over the costs involved. John manages to get in an artful gripe about his latest expense claim and then, uttering his customary, 'Well, another day, another dollar. . .', Bill departs. — 2 7

09.20 – 10.26 During this period, John is primarily concerned with clearing his in-tray – but, as always, the activity is punctuated by a number of 'events':

a Three incoming telephone calls, two of which require Mary's help in digging out filed information. One of the callers is a garrulous individual, and John's usually 4 2 – brief pleasantries are required 3 ½ – to be unduly prolonged. 1½ ½ –

b He makes two phone calls, one of them internal and brief ½ – – in duration. 2½ ¼ –

c Mary interrupts his work with a reminder that he is due to attend the Staff Consultative Committee meeting at 10.30. They briefly discuss the agenda and the likelihood that Mrs Morris, a virago staff member, will table further outlandish proposals. 2 1½ –

John does achieve a goodly amount of work on his in-tray – but, nevertheless, his thoughts do

	tend to stray. He thinks again about the meeting and that argumentative so-and-so, Mrs Morris. Leapfrogging, as only the human mind can do, he entertains further gloomy thoughts on money – recalling that the car is overdue for a service and the wife needs a new coat for the winter. And the probable size of the next telephone bill . . .	41½	–	6¼
10.26 – 10.34	Calling at the loo *en route*, he proceeds to the conference room. The SCC meeting is slightly late in getting under way – and, while waiting, John engages in small-talk with his manager-colleagues.	–	–	8
10.34 – 12.55	As he feared, the meeting proves to be a protracted affair – mainly due to the inability of Charlie Blenkinsop, the sales director and SCC chairman, to control the session and limit discussion to relevant issues. While this is not strictly John's fault, it does mean that much of his time is frittered away on red herrings and needless chit-chat.	86	31	24
12.55 – 13.02	John returns to his office, where he is briefly button-holed by Mary. He discusses a couple of phone messages with her and then departs for lunch.	6½	–	½
13.02 –14.04	Lunch – John's time is his own, and no one is going to carp (I hope) over the fact that he takes two extra minutes. . .	–	–	–
14.04 –14.45	Back at work, he has just started some dictation when the MD comes through on the intercom,			

seeking information and requiring John's presence 'a.s.a.p.' – which means 'p.d.q.' in anyone's language. After a mini-flap, digging through the files, John makes his way to the MD's office, armed with the necessary figures. A period of forty-one minutes is expended as follows:

a	Dictation and fact-finding.	3½	–	–
b	Transit between offices.	–	–	1½
c	Talking turkey with the MD.	24	–	–
d	Listening obediently to the MD pontificate on quite irrelevant issues.	–	7½	–
e	Indulging in pure gossip with the big boss.	–	–	4½

14.45 – 15.11 John returns to his desk all set to complete his dictation, but Mary reminds him that he must phone one of the people who rang up during his absence at the SCC meeting. She obtains the number and, during the ensuing telephone conversation, John learns that he will shortly be receiving a visit from a Department of Health and Social Security official regarding the firm's Statutory Sick Pay records. Being a bit of a 'belt and braces' man, John pops through to the general office to have a word with Mrs Grundy, his personnel clerk. They discuss the SSP situation and, satisfied that all is well (no pun intended), he then proceeds to have a round-robin chat with his five other members of staff. The twenty-six minutes are expended as follows:

a	Telephone call regarding SSP.	3½	–	¼
b	Transit between offices.	–	–	½

31

c	Discussing SSP with Mrs Grundy.	11¼	1½	–
d	Chatting with his staff.	3¼	5¼	½

15.11
– 15.32   Mindful of the need to complete his dictation in time for Mary to type everything up before day-end, John buckles down to the task. The telephone rings once during the period – a call from the sales rep at Ajax Office Supplies, seeking an order. Mary deals with the call while John waits, straining at the leash to complete his dictation.

a	Dictating – interspersed with snippets of chit-chat;	16	2½	1
b	Waiting for Mary, John half-listens to her conversation with the caller, his mind jolted from the task in hand.	–	–	1½

15.32
– 16.10   As Mary cradles the receiver, they are interrupted by the sudden entry of Ken Speare, the works manager, who says that he must have an urgent word with John about the canteen arrangements for the newly instituted twilight shift. While the two men engage in discussion, Mary departs to type out some of the dictation and to fetch tea for them both. The canteen manning problem provokes a lengthy discussion which, happily, stays 'on course' with few irrelevancies creeping in.   35   2   1

16. 10
– 16.31   Hurray! Speare's departure signals an uninterrupted session of twenty-one minutes, during which John completes his dictation.   20   ½   ½

16.31 – 17.13		During this period, John spends his time as follows:			
	a	Making a phone call to the canteen supervisor, outlining his proposals for the twilight shift catering.	3¼	–	–
	b	Making a phone call to his garage to book a service for his car.	–	–	2½
	c	Phoning Ken Speare to confirm the canteen arrangements.	1½	–	–
	d	Checking and confirming the weekly record of overtime for his staff.	2	–	–
	e	Dealing with an incoming call from Securicor concerning the factory night-guard.	1¼	–	–
	f	Working solidly on his in-tray.	27	–	–
	g	Visiting the loo, complete with wash and brush-up.	–	–	4½
17.13 – 17.32		This period is expended as follows:			
	a	Mary brings in the finished correspondence for signing. John, realizing that it is too late for the normal office despatch, asks her to post one particularly important letter on her way home. Then, with a brief word or two, he bids Mary goodnight.	3	½	½
	b	The muted hubbub of staff leaving the building prompts him to sit back with a sigh of relief – and cogitate on the day's work.	1	1	–
	c	He drafts a memo on the new canteen arrangements – Mary can crack it off first thing in the morning.	12	–	–
	d	He clears up his desk.	–	1	–

17.32 – 17.55	John is about to quit his ofice when Bill, the accountant, pops his head round the door. With the opening comment, 'John, I think you'd like to see this', he hands John a preliminary budget for the forthcoming six-month period. The two men sit down and discuss the figures, particularly those concerned with administation, which have been subjected to the usual pruning. For the umpteenth time, John argues his case . . .	21	1	1
17.55	And that's that. Our worthy manager grabs his briefcase and, conscious that he's got away with an early finish for once, sets out from the office, homeward bound for the wife and a tasty pot-roast.			
	TOTALS IN MINUTES	363	65	73

Note: Although John is an imaginary character, all his listed activities and associated timings have been derived from observations of an actual manager at work.

Let us now examine those 'totals in minutes':

363 minutes of 'actual work' Plainly, this is the stuff for which John is paid – the duties and tasks of his employment.

65 minutes of 'work-related obligations' This is the 'grey area' of John's (and anyone's) employment – the countless activities that we are all required to perform to ensure all-round success at the job. Thus, John's deliberate conversation with his staff (or, to be precise, the greater part of what he had to say and discuss) falls safely into this category, since by chatting pleasantly to the good souls of the general office, he was doing what any proficient manager would do to motivate and encourage his or her subordinates. However, and here's the crunch, there obviously comes a point when any such activity tends to decay into superfluous and unproductive chit-chat, or whatever. All of which brings us to the third category . . .

73 minutes of 'leisure at work' And here we have it – the total period of time spent by John, *and by all of us,* pursuing strictly leisure or personal activities – the wholly unproductive segment of the working day.

Whoa back, there! Before you start hammering me with outraged assertions that man is not a machine and all that jazz, just consider this business of 'leisure at work' in a little more depth. If, just for illustration, we assume that John's salary is £10,000 per annum for a working year of 240 days, with each day comprising seven and a half hours' work, his time (ignoring, if we dare, such weighty things as National Insurance and other employers' contributions) can be costed as follows:

One day:	£41.66
One hour:	£5.55
One minute:	9.25p

Of course, it could be said by some coldly efficient, ink-for-blood boffin that, on the day we've just examined, the Excelsior Snug-Fit Truss Company paid John the munificent sum of £6.75 for the privilege of using the loo, striding the corridors of power and gossiping his head off. Aye, well, it may be right and proper to think along those lines when controlling the hapless minions on the factory floor, but I'd like to think that managers worth their salt are never, ever, subjected to such infernal skulduggery.

So what's the point, do I hear you ask? All right then, let's get down to the meat in the sandwich . . . While my purpose in setting out John's day in all its gory detail is most certainly to emphasize the truth of that old adage 'Time costs money', I have absolutely no intention of urging a nit-picking crack-down on visits to the loo and so forth. The point is one of basic principle: namely, just how many of us really do get down to the vital business of examining in detail the composition of the working day? You know the answer as well as I do – precious few. But we're going to change all that – and we'll make a start by simply acknowledging that the first step along this very commendable road is to develop an eagle-eyed awareness of the pound signs in each and every activity.

Self-tutorial

Exercise 2

This is where you'll need those notes from the first exercise which, as I'm sure you will recall, asked you to study Tom Bosworth's day at work and decide if and when he contrived to waste his time. Take a candid look at your jottings, and head straight for the doghouse if, in tackling the task, you failed (forgot is a kinder word) to think objectively in terms of setting some priorities – say, for example:

Priority 1 Very urgent and highly important activities to which Tom should have given his immediate and undivided attention.

Priority 2 Very urgent but not so important activities, which, if Tom was pushed for time, he should have delegated to a suitably experienced member of his staff.

Priority 3 Not so urgent but highly important activities which, if pressed for time, Tom should have delegated so that, at the very least, preliminary ground would have been broken and a start made.

Priority 4 Those activities which, lacking urgency or importance, Tom should (if necessary) have shelved, ignored or passed to someone else.

For this exercise, have a shot at allocating one of the above priorities to each of Tom's activities in the following summary. You may find it useful to refer to the full text of 'his day' and, of course, those very copious notes . . .

	Activity	**Priority**
1	His start-of-the-day check to see that everyone was present and correct.	_____
2	His action to obtain a stand-in clerk from Accounts.	_____
3	His discussion with John Napper, the production manager.	_____
4	His counselling session with Bill Dyer, the clerk.	_____
5	His work on the draft monthly sales report.	_____
6	His last-minute 'swotting-up' for the bi-monthly management meeting.	_____

36

7   His late-morning, 'customary' round of the
    department.   _____

8   His telephone conversation with his wife, which
    resulted in his late arrival at the sales meeting. _____

9   His hard work during the meeting to convince the
    sales reps that the company had no intention of
    cutting back on its sales force.   _____

You can check your findings against the notes at the end of this self-tutorial.

Exercise 3

Before we go any further, sit back with your calculator and work out exactly how much you get paid per working day, hour and minute. This is not quite so silly as it may appear – for, if we are to make a serious, in-depth study of the effective management of time, it is vital to gain a conscious appreciation of the fact that *time, to each one of us, is a finite resource.* One sure method of reinforcing this necessary attitude of mind is to face up to the sixty-thousand dollar question:

How much do *you* cost to do what you do?

Memory-prodder 2

Having placed a price on your head, closet yourself in the privacy of your own mind and consider with the utmost self-candour:

- When you attend meetings and burble on and on, held spellbound by the loquacity of your own voice, *how much does it cost?*

- When you engage in those cosy, ritual natters with your colleagues, taking a bite out of the morning to pass the time of day, *how much does it cost?*

- When you're working like fury at your desk, and bingo, that spritely mind slips off to sylvan thoughts of the man or woman in your life, or how much you're likely to get when Aunt Agatha finally turns her toes up, *how much does it cost?*

- When you are sounding off to your staff, and your pearly words of wisdom are knee-deep in waffle, *how much does it cost?*

- When you are drafting a stroke of written genius, and have just torn up the seventh stab at the opening paragraph, *how much does it cost?*

- When you are on the telephone, and you allow irrelevant little chit-chat niceties to take up more than half the call, *how much – with telephone charges added in – does it cost?*

You know, it really is worth repeating

How much do you cost to do what you do?

Notes on Exercise 2

Remembering that nothing in the art of management can be a '2 + 2 = 4' situation (which, of course, is why the boffins constantly remind us that we are dealing with an 'organic' subject), check to see how your elected priorities compare with the following:

1   Firstly, as the poet said, why keep a dog and bark yourself? Tom would have done a whole heap better to rely on Mary, his supervisor, to report any absentees. Such routine, run-of-the-mill tasks should have been delegated to her way back – and probably were. From the limited list of options how does *Priority 4* grab you?

2   It would not be nit-picking to accuse Tom of lacking faith in Mary's prowess as a supervisor. Since she had already completed her own re-shuffle of work, our hero should have asked her if, in fact, a temporary stand-in was actually necessary before going ahead to scrounge one. Poor Mary, it seems that she has quite a lot to put up with – and Tom is guilty of failing to recognize, at best, a *Priority 4* activity.

3   From the scant information available, you'll probably agree that Tom was quite right to deal promptly and efficiently with Napper's queries on a *Priority 1* basis.

4   Nothing short of a thumping great crisis should prevent any manager from listening to a subordinate's cry for help – and, once again, Tom was quite right to deal with Dyer's problem as a

Priority 1 task. Having done so, he would have been wise to check, first, why the clerk had not seen fit to approach his supervisor in the first instance, and, second, if he had done exactly that, why Mary had failed to examine the problem and make her own recommendations.

5   If, as we may fairly assume, the completion of the sales report was a highly personal task, then Tom really had no option but to get the thing finished as soon as possible – a *Priority 1* activity which, because life is like that at work, was bound to clash with other top priorities. Incidentally, it is perhaps worth querying why Tom had to spend so much of his time correcting a typed draft – or, more to the point, we should question the standard of his original work on the report. Far too many managers either draft or dictate in a thoroughly haphazard fashion, giving no thought to the cart-load of typing thus produced, and caring little about the fact that, once the poor secretary concerned has bashed it all out, the work will require nothing short of a carve-up to make it presentable. So, posing the obvious, between-the-ribs question: how good is *your* drafting and dictation?

6   There is no delegation or shelving possible with this one – if Tom needed to swot up for the meeting, then it's a *Priority 1* task. The point is, did he – by negligence or design – leave this very important activity until literally the last (and nearly always the most unsuitable) moment?

7   This one's debatable, but probably *Priority 1*. Tom's decision to make his customary round of the department when he did depended on, among other things, his current state of play work-wise and, of course, any knowledge he may have had of impending or actual hiccups in the sales office (but remembering that he does have a supervisor out there . . .).

8   Yes, this is an unfair one. We all have other priorities in life and, provided Tom did not unduly prolong the telephone conversation with his wife, I, for one, would not like to cast the first stone.

9   Dear me, in view of what was to transpire later in the day, Tom was on a very sticky wicket in thus encouraging his salesmen. But the poor guy didn't have a clue that his working world was about to be so severely shaken – clearly, it was a *Priority 1*, motivation-type task.

How did you fare? If this little exercise gave you food for thought, why, all well and good, it achieved its objective!

Apropos of absolutely nothing

Thinking of variations in the speed of rotation of the Earth (which, of course, you are), did you know that tidal friction causes a progressive increase in the length of the day of about .001 of a second per century?

Good grief, more unpaid overtime – without even realizing it!

3 A stiff dose of self-management

And thou, who didst the stars and sunbeams know,
Self-schooled, self-scanned, self-honoured, self-secure
Didst tread on earth unguessed at. Better so!

Matthew Arnold,
Shakespeare

An executive guru at whose knee I once sat was very fond of reminding all and sundry that good management, like the proverbial charity, begins at home. Closing in on his chosen victim with a penetrating, almost hypnotic stare, he'd proclaim his wise dictum with such emphasis that whoever was in his line of fire felt compelled to ask for an explanation – which, of course, was exactly what the old chap was after. Settling himself in his chair, he would preface what always turned out to be a rattling good mini-lecture with the words, 'See here, laddie, before anyone can entertain a hope of managing others effectively, he must be able to manage himself . . .Can *you* manage *your*self?'.

On the odd occasion, the object of his attention would possess enough self-confidence or brash extroversion to reply in the affirmative – and, more often than not, would wish within minutes that he hadn't. Sucking the guy's brains with the ease of a vacuum cleaner, the guru would very swiftly establish that, far from being a proficient self-manager, the poor clod was a bumbling amateur at the game. All of which brings me to this chapter's opening point: despite all our dearly held beliefs and protestations, most of us are pretty damned poor at the art of managing ourselves, let alone others.

There are three principal ingredients that go towards the making of a first-rate self-management pie:

1   Self-discipline

2   A methodical outlook

3   The ability to organize time and effort

The elusive quality of self-discipline

During the early stages of World War II, when the army was desperately seeking large numbers of commissioned officers with which to swell the ranks of its regular elite, the red-tabbed general staff came up with what to them was the conception of the century – War Office Selection Boards. 'Wosbies', as they came to be known, may best be described as hastily strung-together administrative sausage machines, designed and run by a near-fatal admix of civil servants, psychologists and, of course, suitably vetted army officers (the fact that no one gave much thought to vetting the psychologists virtually guaranteed some striking examples of selection mayhem). As I have intimated, the Wosbies had but one purpose in life – to dig among the human rockery and come up with moderately clean-limbed (there was a war on), clear-thinking and stiff-upper-lipped potential officers. Not surprisingly, much of the amateur assessment knavery that went on behind Wosbie closed doors was devoted to the detection and appraisal of *self-discipline* in candidates – for if a fellow has to lead chaps into situations where they're likely to get their heads blown off, he must have what it takes to control himself and, above all else, set an example. Well, while the selection boards employed methods which were little short of witchcraft in attaining their aim, there is no doubt at all that they were dead right in electing for self-discipline as a prerequisite in the make-up of a leader. I know it to be true – and, more to the point, so do you.

But there's a mighty big snag . . . If, as is vitally necessary, we make a resolution to look inwards and assess our individual qualities of self-discipline, we are in imminent danger of donning mental blinkers and looking at the task in much the same way as some of us might regard BO – only too eager to detect it in others, but remaining steadfastly blind to our own, sorely afflicted state. Who, even in the privacy of their heart of hearts, is frank enough to admit that, yes, they are lacking in this or that aspect of self-discipline? Gosh, I'm sorry, reader, I underestimated your strength of character - you are! Absolutely splendid, but do you possess the indomitable spirit, if given the prod, to do something about those weak areas? You do? Fair enough, here we go – eyes down and looking for trouble in the self-discipline mill.

A self-appraisal in self-discipline

The drill is quite straightforward: bearing in mind that massive strength of character, plonk your mark where it hurts most . . .

		True				Untrue	
1	When I'm feeling tetchy or otherwise out-of-sorts, I do not succeed in hiding the fact from others.	1	2	3	4	5	6
2	And such bad moods affect my relationships with my colleagues . . .	1	2	3	4	5	6
3	. . . and with my subordinates.	1	2	3	4	5	6
4	Try as I might, domestic and other out-of-work worries affect my attitudes at work . . .	1	2	3	4	5	6
5	. . . and the quality of my work . . .	1	2	3	4	5	6
6	. . . and my output.	1	2	3	4	5	6
7	I find it difficult to concentrate on boring, repetitive tasks.	1	2	3	4	5	6
8	I react strongly to bad moods in others, in that I am adversely affected by them.	1	2	3	4	5	6
9	While I try not to let it show, I often get into a 'mental panic' when under stress.	1	2	3	4	5	6
10	But I'm afraid it does show.	1	2	3	4	5	6
11	Given provocation at work, yes, I have been known to lose my temper . . .	1	2	3	4	5	6
12	. . . and, if I am totally frank, sometimes without provocation.	1	2	3	4	5	6

Note, if you will, that I'm not attempting to present you with a list of the mental abilities required to attain the nirvana of self-discipline. If you haven't picked up the odd clue from your stab

45

at the self-appraisal, why, there's no way you'll derive any benefit from a selection of superlatives. Suffice it to say – and, come to think of it, an anonymous Greek philosopher has said it already – *know thyself*.

And next – a methodical outlook and approach to one's work

You can't have one without the other. It normally follows that an individual who lacks self-discipline is also 'unmethodical' – and, who knows, a determined effort to correct the latter could well bring about a resounding improvement in the former weakness. It's jolly well worth a try.

The most successful managers, those thin-on-the-ground, dynamically efficient and inspiring types whom we all envy like stink, always give the appearance of being totally unhurried, totally unworried and totally in control. Strictly between ourselves, this is because Fate has given them the sheer good sense to see, obey and profit by the *Three Big Rules for Adopting a Methodical Approach*.

Rule 1   Create and maintain a strict and sensible schedule of work

Success in following this rule alone will place your feet firmly on the road to good self-discipline – but, just as important, it will result in a massive reduction of the time spent on all those non-essential fripperies at work.

Rule 2   Pinpoint and allocate proper attention to the important tasks

We're back to the question of allocating *priorities* and adequate time for the completion of tasks.

Rule 3   Allow adequate time for constructive thinking and planning

However humble his situation, however humble his task, there is no manager alive who can afford to ignore the vital business of thinking and planning ahead; those who do are not, in fact, alive - they are the undead of the executive world.

And lastly – the ability to really organize time and effort

It's likely that your first glance at the title of this book – or, for that matter, your very first thought about the effective management of time – produced a pretty swift conclusion: 'Ah, yes, that's all about keeping a diary of one's daily doings – I mean, it has to be, doesn't it?' And you would have been quite correct. Since time is infinitely more valuable than money and, as if that were not enough, *is a constantly wasting asset*, any manager who fails to budget the precious commodity is being foolhardy in the extreme – for, whether the poor idiot knows it or not, he is literally spitting in the face of Fate. I make no apology at all for bawling in your ear: IT'S NOT ENOUGH TO SPORT A MICKEY MOUSE, BLEEPING WRISTWATCH AND OWN A PIGSKIN APPOINTMENTS DIARY! As you read these words, even as you draw that breath, your Current Account at the Bank of Time is being further depleted by an unremittingly expensive Direct Debit – and, whatever your power or status in life, you cannot redress the balance. All you can hope to do is ensure that your waning capital is spent wisely, and this can only be achieved by making probably the most important decision that's ever been yours to make: namely, *to budget time and effort as if your life depended on it – which it does*.

In the next chapter we're going to get to grips with ways and means of doing exactly that, but, for the moment, sticking like glue to the 'slowly, slowly, catch'ee monkey' philosophy, I'm merely asking that you prepare for the hard work to come by familiarizing yourself with the *Four Big Rules For Budgeting Time and Effort*.

Rule 1 List all the jobs that have to be done, and group them by type

Rule 2 Determine the order in which they are to be tackled

Rule 3 Apportion time to each task

Rule 4 And, last but certainly not least, establish a fully effective self-monitoring and checking system

And that, in essence, is self-management – attained via the painstaking process of acquiring self-discipline, a methodical outlook and an ability to organize time and effort. However, just to rub in the fact that life isn't always such a bowl of cherries, I'd like to provide you with some gory reminders of what can happen when, very sadly, self-management is only conspicuous by its absence.

A behind-the-scenes peep at a personal file

For many of us, our executive progress is signposted and, whether we like it or not, determined by the outcome of periodic performance appraisals. In the more progressive outfits (which, I hope, includes the one in which you work), the appraisals are of the open, discussion-encouraged variety, but there are still many organizations that favour the worrying and secretive business of 'closed' appraisal – when, quite often, an ill-performing victim knows nothing of his fate until the moment when the bullet thuds into his back. Doug Williams, an area sales manager, works for such an organization and, right now, just as he is happily slogging away in his territory, the document that will trigger his personal bullet is being read by his managing director . . .

The Dudley Copple Group	Staff Confidential

MANAGEMENT PERFORMANCE APPRAISAL

Name: D J Williams	Company/Dept: DCS – UK Sales
Post: Area Sales Manager (SW)	Time in post: 1 year 3 months
Period: 1 April 83 – 31 March 84	Reporter: C H Robinson Director UK Sales

NARRATIVE REPORT FOR PERIOD

In terms of general personality, enthusiasm and willingness to work hard, Williams has more than justified my faith in his ability to make a success of this appointment. Bearing in mind that he was promoted fairly early in his career with the Company and, as an inevitable consequence, was regarded (to say the least) with some doubt by the members of his team, he very quickly established himself as a caring, albeit demanding, manager. I cannot but praise the manner in which he gathered up the loose threads, as it were, and motivated all concerned to greater and more sustained effort – a fact which is confirmed by the increase in SW area sales over the period of this report.

However, having stated this, and having made due allowances for the demands of a fairly exacting post, I must confess to very serious disappointment regarding other and vital aspects of this young manager's performance which, in my view, call into question his continued usefulness to the Company. Firstly and most important, since his appointment the efficiency of the SW area sales office as an administrative unit has shown a marked deterioration. Weekly, monthly and other returns – which, prior to Williams taking over, were notable for their accuracy and timely submission – are now rarely without error and, despite my personal intervention, consistently late in arrival at HO. Since there have been no staff shortages in the SW office during the period, it is difficult to lay the blame for this deterioration at any other than the manager's door. Williams knows my feelings on this but I am bound to admit that, despite my several warnings, he appears to have done little or nothing to bring about an improvement. I am equally perturbed by the standard of his personal written work, which very often reflects ill-organized and hasty composition – and, where his monthly sales reports are concerned, a propensity to lateness in submission.

I have made a point of visiting Williams regularly during the period and, on two occasions, called to see him without prior warning. On all these occasions, and more particularly when I turned up unannounced, I was less than impressed with his general efficiency as an administrator. There is no doubt in my mind that he lacks the ability to organize his working day, with the consequence that he is continually trying (and failing) to tackle too many tasks at once – a fact which, judging by the general climate now existing at the SW office, does not pass unnoticed by his staff.

As I have stated, I cannot fault Williams's motivational efforts where the salesmen in the field are concerned, or, for that matter, deny that sales have increased. However, with the best will in the world, I cannot allow these successes to blind me to the fact that, unless I go to the length of engaging an office administrator to undertake what is rightfully this manager's desk-work (and this is out of the question), things at the SW office will deteriorate even further. I therefore have no option but to consider a more efficient replacement for Williams as soon as possible.

(Signed)

C H Robinson
Director UK Sales

Poor old Williams – or would you say that he had sown the seeds of his own misfortune? Before you plonk your rubber stamp on his demise, just pause for a second and ponder your own, real-life situation . . . Could it be that, somewhere up the line, there is a senior manager thinking in similarly nasty terms about *your* overall performance? Do you think that your difficulties in organizing time and effort have, in fact, been noticed by some such highly placed vulture? Crikey, read on!

He was a good chap, but . . .

For my second example of a guy who didn't even know the meaning of good self-management, let alone practise it, I'd like to tell you about Gary and how, in the fullness of time, his career was scuppered by a series of high-velocity bullets fired from above.

As a student, Gary was one of Nature's plodders and, for all that he found his degree course a hard nut to crack, his dogged perseverance earned him a fairly commendable BA in Business Studies and, probably just as important, a management-trainee post within a large and go-ahead organization. I suppose it would be something of a kindness to say that his particular efficiency-rot set in over a period of time, but I'm afraid that wasn't the case. Pitched fairly precipitately from a world of academic routine into the comparative maelstrom of the workplace – where, even as a trainee, he was required to demonstrate personal initiative in organizing and implementing his various activities – our lad was beguiled right from the start by those dreaded sirens of good management, *time wasters*.

Before continuing with the sad story of Gary's downfall, let us be military-minded and conduct a short, sharp appraisal of the enemy. One handy way to do this is to examine time wasters in the context of the basic 'functions of management', which were first set out in 1916 by the redoubtable Henry Fayol, a French industrialist and management wizard, as follows:

Forecasting and planning
Organizing
Commanding
Co-ordinating
Controlling

Plainly, there are many variations on this theme of management functions, but Fayol's list is as good as any for the purpose of illustrating some typical time wasters. Take a good look at them, for it's not only the ducklings of the management pool who succumb to their lure – *but, to some extent or other, every single one of us*. By the way, in casting an eagle eye over the examples, stretch your mind a little and add your personal weaknesses to the collection . . .

Function	Typical time wasters
Forecasting and planning	Failing to establish/observe aims and priorities.
	Failing to recognize and take due account of likely conditions/constraints.
	Failing to establish realistic criteria.
	Trying to tackle too much at once.
	Honey-bee thinking – flitting from one project/subject to another.
	Pure and simple daydreaming.
Organizing	Failing to distinguish between authority and responsibility.
	Trying to organize others when one's personal working life is disorganized.
	Trying to organize when suffering under the conflicting dictums of several bosses.
	Failing to see the wood for the trees.
Commanding	Failing to communicate one's wishes in an effective manner.
	Delegating improperly and ineffectively.
	When issuing instructions, failing to motivate staff to give of their best.
	Tunnel vision – failing to heed the often common-sense suggestions of others.
Co-ordinating	Failing to ensure that given projects do not clash or interfere with other commitments.
	Failing to ensure that staff are in a position to report, liaise and, if necessary, combine their efforts.
Controlling	Failing to ensure that adequate feedback is created and maintained.
	Failing to impose satisfactory standards of performance.
	Allowing distractions to erode one's overall control and/or control of specific situations.
	Succumbing to the temptation of over-controlling – nagging 'em to death.

Returning to the story of Gary, his initial undoing as a trainee was brought about by a combination of his pleasant, easy-going manner and sheer inexperience. Sent hither and thither within the organization on a series of 'working by experience' assignments and, to a large extent, encouraged by the ne'er-do-wells who lurk in the crevices of any company, he swiftly developed a penchant for idle chit-chat. It wasn't very long before his reputation as a gossiping time waster reached the ears of his boss – together with the more damning information that Gary (probably out of sheer ignorance and a desire to 'keep his end up' during the many chat sessions) had uttered this and that disloyal comment about his employer. Righteously concerned that he had a potential viper in the nest, the boss did for the first time what he should have been doing all along and went through Gary's overall performance with a fine tooth-comb. Sadly, the appraisal revealed that the lad had not worked very effectively; and, choosing to ignore the fact that, at the very least, this was partly due to the company's inept training methods, he was 'invited' to resign. Knowing he had precious little choice in the matter, Gary did exactly that and found himself in the invidious position of being unemployed, with nothing but a potentially poor reference to back his efforts in landing another job.

Make no mistake, Gary had no illusions about his performance while in the service of this first, crucial employer. He freely admitted that he'd chit-chatted unwisely and often only worked at half-cock; and, being a decent chap at heart, was absolutely determined to do a whole heap better next time – if, that is, he got the chance. The weeks of unemployment stretched into months and, getting really desperate, Gary started looking at the honey-pot of highly paid, tax-free contract jobs in the ubiquitous Third World. And, sure enough, after a series of unsuccessful stabs, he was finally accepted for a post as 'administrative supervisor' within a Kuwaiti industrial outfit. And, reader, in the unlikely event you have tears, prepare to shed them now . . .

Picture the situation. Still feeling guilty and ashamed over his initial *denouement*, Gary found himself in a job where the philosophy was simple: either work like a dingbat and earn the big money, or move over and make room for someone else. So, armed with his degree course knowledge and miniscule actual experience, the newly appointed supervisor set to with a vengeance – and lasted just over three months. In what amounted to a frenzy of activity, Gary not only committed nearly every time-wasting sin in the book, but also contrived to put the literal touch of death on his relations with subordinates, peers and seniors alike. You've probably guessed the root cause of his trouble, but let's place it on record. Pushed by a frantic desire to 'make good', to be the very epitome of a young, thrusting and super-efficient manager, he hoisted himself on the petard of his own, gross inexperience and suffered the almost inevitable consequence, dismissal.

When last I heard of him, Gary, now a dispirited shadow of his earlier self, had been in and out of his fifth, terribly low-grade job – and I feel nothing but pessimism for his future. Ah, yes, it's terribly easy to say 'But he had it all coming to him' and, because he's not kith and kin, cast his story aside. If that, reader, is your somewhat justifiable reaction, then here's a postscript – for your eyes only. Promotion, redeployment or taking on another job places very many bright-eyed and bushy-tailed management 'careerists' in exactly Gary's situation in Kuwait. Lest you doubt this assertion, think of Dr Laurence J. Peter and his brilliantly perceptive *Peter Principle*, now accepted world-wide as a basic and unpalatable fact of management life:

> 'In a hierarchy every employee tends to rise to his maximum level of incompetence'.

Do you have burgeoning self-confidence in the manner in which you are tackling *all* the aspects of that new assignment – or, even more to the point, *all* the facets of the job which you've held for some time now? Well, do you?

Exactly how good a self-manager are you?

Self-tutorial

Exercise 4

Cast your mind back a few pages to that self-appraisal exercise. Go on, of course you remember it – the one on self-discipline that caused you to tell some whoppers . . . The appraisal was concerned with a number of 'items' (or, if you're a die-hard glutton for textbook terminology, traits), which I guess can be summarized as follows:

1   Failure to conceal 'bad moods' from others.
2   Allowing such moods to affect one's relationships with colleagues . . .

3   . . . and one's relationships with subordinates.
4   Allowing domestic and other worries to affect one's attitudes at work . . .
5   . . . and one's quality of work . . .
6   . . . and one's work output.
7   Difficulty in concentrating on boring, repetitive tasks.
8   Strong, adverse reaction to bad moods in others.
9   Inclination to 'mentally panic' when under stress.
10   Failing to conceal such panic from others.
11   Inclination to lose temper when provoked.
12   Inclination to lose temper without actual provocation from others.

Weigh each item in your mind with particular regard to:

- the manner in which it affects and shapes your own 'work personality';
- the manner in which it affects and shapes the work personalities of your seniors, peers and colleagues.

This is an exercise in pinpointing specific instances of 'aggro' at work arising from self-discipline weaknesses in yourself and others. Knuckle down to the task and examine root causes, effects and, where realistic, possible solutions. Above all, tutor yourself to think objectively about these disturbing ripples – and, maybe for the first time in your working life, analyse them.

Memory-prodder 3

How much of this chapter has *really stuck*? If, as you profess, you are gifted with reasonable (or marvellous!) abilities of self-management, you will need little reminding of its three principal ingredients:

- Self-discipline
- A methodical outlook
- The ability to organize time and effort

Okay, clever-clogs – so now define them.

More apropos of absolutely nothing

While the age of dear old Mother Earth is at least 4,500 million years, the differentiation of apes from the ancestors of man only began some 25 million years ago and, as we all know to our cost, is by no means complete.

4 So what d'you do there, anyway?

> Not only is there but one way of DOING things rightly,
> but there is only one way of SEEING them, and that is
> seeing the whole of them.
>
> John Ruskin,
> *The Two Paths*

Ho, yes, we all know in our innermost thoughts exactly what we do
at work, don't we? The trouble is, if someone was able to plug into
our mental recesses, he'd find that what we often tell *others* we do
is not necessarily an accurate reflection of those thoughts – simply
because the privy chamber of our mind is sacrosanct, inviolable
and dead private. Well, guess what, I'm armed with just such a
plug, and I aim to use it. If, perchance, I link up with your private
circuit, try not to flinch.

'Do you mind? My thoughts are not for publication, for the reason that
nobody where I work would be willing to accept the simple truth that, if it
wasn't for my personal efforts, the whole outfit would collapse in no time
flat. I tackle every single task that comes my way with verve,
determination and considerable skill – and although people never seem
to appreciate the fact, it's my loyalty, logicality and level of expertise that
they should all be trying to match. All of which, of course, is why I'm only
reading this book for lack of something better to do – believe you me, I
don't really need to plough through it . . .

'I do far too much . . . The trouble is, they use the constant excuse that they
can't afford to employ more staff – with the result that I'm really a
manager-cum-dogsbody, and it doesn't work. You can bet your life that as
soon as I get my teeth into something worthwhile, or something really
urgent, the interruptions'll start. I'm getting heartily sick of it all – I reckon
I'm a pretty good manager, but I never get the chance to prove it!
Someone else always gets the praise – I just get the kicks.'

'Look, when it comes to the crunch, I suppose I don't really mind doing all
the jobs I've got on my slop-chit, but they sure do grind me down at times
– and the last thing I want to take home every night is a headache. So,
although I'm damned if I'd admit it out loud, I play it safe and put on a bit
of an act . . . Y'know what I mean, give 'em the impression I'm always busy
– and certainly too busy to take on anything else . . . It's amazing, really, it
always seems to work! Look after Number One, that's what I say.'

'I do a fair day's work for a pretty mean day's pay – and that just about says it all. I've got what I think is a good approach to my work, inasmuch as I tackle everything that comes along in a logical way and without getting into a flap . . . I don't think anyone could accuse me of falling down on the job, and I'd be pretty upset if someone did.'

'Oh, God, I'm scared . . . I do my level best at work, but I never get any praise or even a thank you for my efforts. I know they all talk about me behind my back – oh, yes, I can tell – and I'm certain they're out to get me in the end.'

'What do I do at work? Ha, that's an easy one – as little as possible! They couldn't care less about me, and I wouldn't give tuppence for them – they're an absolute shower. Anyway, there are more things to life than work, and I aim to enjoy 'em!'

So there we are – a small selection of subjective, innermost thoughts for your digestion. The trouble is, if one gives any consideration at all to the question of what one does at work, nine times out of ten it's a fleeting and inaccurate appraisal – a kind of self-commiserating balm, to be applied at will. This being the case, before proceeding to the vital business of analysing what we *should* all be doing at work, allow me to put the proverbial knife in . . . What, if anything, do you think of *your* activities at work – and having thus thought, why in blazes don't you do something about it? Come to think of it, now's your chance!

In order to come anywhere near to getting to grips with the vital business of time-effective performance, it is necessary for the manager to examine the many and various functions which, in sum, comprise the duties of his appointment. One very handy method is, quite simply, to analyse work under four main headings:

- Routine activities
- People activities
- 'Thinking'
- Problem-solving

Routine activities

The danger with this category is that, unless one is very careful, it will become a dustbin for all the odds and bobs of the daily round and thus defeat the whole object of the exercise. Having said that, there is a plethora of repetitive duties which, being carried out on a daily, weekly or other regular basis, must be classified under this heading. For this initial carve-up (and at the risk of insulting your intelligence), suffice it to say that chores like reading and actioning correspondence, checking procedures and rendering returns are all routine activities.

People activities

If your immediate reaction at the sight of this category was something akin to 'That's the personnel manager's job, not mine', then it's transparently clear that you're dead from the neck up – but it wasn't, was it? Being a caring, thinking individual, you will know that it is the duty of every single manager to never let a minute pass without actively considering and striving for:

1   Manpower efficiency.
2   The good welfare and well-being of one's staff.
3   The full implementation of legal obligations to one's people.

It is thus fitting – nay, essential – that 'people activities' should be afforded a prime place in our preliminary analysis of managers' work.

Thinking

It was a Charles Dickens character (Coavinses in *Bleak House*) who said, 'Think! I've got enough to do, and little enough to get for it, without thinking.' Thank God, few managers share that view – I hope. The whole business of making time for constructive, logical and purposeful thinking has to be a priority in any executive's struggle for optimum efficiency. Unfortunately, and as we all know to our cost, there is such a thing as Sod's Law – and this immutable legislation ensures that the process of 'thinking' constitutes one of the biggest traps to all but the most clear-headed in our midst. But take heart, for we'll come to all that in a later chapter.

Problem-solving

If, like me, you find it impossible to begin work without a big, bracing cuppa, you will know that it is not for your general refreshment that you take those grateful sips – but, rather, as a form of anaesthetic against the problems that, like vultures, are likely to be pecking at your flesh. At the start of each day, there will be some which you know about and which require your attention, and (remembering Sod's Law) others will arise during the course of your umpteen hours' penance. Clearly, there will be precious little in the way of efficiency unless we budget for time in which to cope with known and unexpected problems – and, since crystal balls are notoriously unreliable in the hands of the average manager, allocating time for the latter contingencies becomes something of a so-and-so. But, my hearties, there is a way, and we'll be having a good, long look at it.

All right then, where do we go from here?

As I've already intimated, detailed examinations of the four main categories of management activity are going to take up a fair chunk of our attention. As a sop to your liking for a methodical approach (without which you'll be done for), the plan of battle is as follows:

Chapter 5   We'll attack the question of *routine* duties at work.
Chapter 6   Then, having tasted blood, we'll carry out a crafty pincer movement on the much-maligned business of all those *people activities*.
Chapter 7   Followed by a foray into the bug-ridden and murky world of 'thinking', and . . .
Chapter 8   . . . a good stab at problem-solving.

But hold on – not so fast!   Before we plunge in at the deep end, I have to put you through that most beloved of all armed forces' exams, the FFI. If you are an ex-service veteran, you will immediately recognize this sterling abbreviation; but, just in case you were not so privileged, the letters stand for 'Free From Infection' – and, no, I'm not going to go into details. Suffice it to say that this FFI isn't concerned with checking your health in respect of dhobi's itch, Bengal rot or Calcutta crabs – but, far more important, your relative freedom from GBMD, the Great British Management Disease.

There are four highly toxic pathogens symptomatic of the GBMD and, if you're to stand any chance at all of becoming time-effective, we must ensure that your executive bloodstream is free of each and every one of them.

Laziness

Sheer laziness – the disinclination of the manager to get off his mental butt – is more endemic in our ranks than we care to think. When, for instance, you see a character sitting motionless at his desk, staring with hypnotic intensity into the middle distance, why, yes, he could be immersed in laudable and work-relevant thought, but it's also an odds-on chance that the miserable creature is simply switched off. You know, although indolence and its first cousin apathy are usually easy to spot, it's quite extraordinary how many lazy managers continue and even flourish in their jobs without getting a swift bullet for their sins.

While I am sure you are a veritable hive of industry, with bags of metaphorical fire in your belly, do remember that laziness is terribly infectious. If you have the misfortune to be squatting in an unrewarding or boring appointment (and, in particular, if you are cursed with a streak of selfishness), then the scene is set for laziness to rear its deceptively attractive head. If, deep down, you are a frightened manager – scared of your organization, your job, or some of the people involved – then, again, you are a sitting target for the indolence bug.

You should also remember that however and whenever the scourge strikes, its arrival is usually prefaced by one or other of the classic 'openers':

'Oh hell, why should I . . .'

'It's not worth the candle . . .'

'Why bother . . .'

'Let someone else do it . . .'

Be truly honest with yourself, if not with me. How do *you* score in the laziness stakes?

That dreaded bug – grasshopping

Cast your mind back to 'John's day at work' in Chapter 2. Do you recall how he arrived early at the office, all eager-beaver and full of determination to get in some work before the telephone started to ring? And can you remember what, in fact, transpired? Having started on his in-tray, bingo, his mind did a glorious hop, skip and a jump, and he started thinking about everything under the sun except the tasks in hand. That, as we know full well, is grasshopping . . .

Picture Mr Manager-Willie sitting at his desk, and, equipping yourself with telepathic powers, tune in to his train of thought:

'Thank God, that's the letters signed – Mary'll be coming in soon to collect 'em . . . where's that wretched report . . . ah, yes, here it is . . . now, let me see – I've got to make some kind of a decision on who's to attend this next skive in London . . . one thing's for sure, it won't be me – George made it quite clear he didn't want me to go . . . I wonder why – he must realize I haven't had a day away from the office in months . . . but who else in the department can I send? . . . more to the point, who deserves to go? I do! . . . was Jean right this morning when she said that George was a bit cool the other night? . . . I didn't notice anything wrong – we gave him a damned good meal, for goodness sake! . . . in fact, that steak was the best we've had in ages – must go to that butcher more often . . . yes, perhaps Jean's right, after all – I must speak to her about George when I get home . . . God, what was it she asked me to get from the chemists on the way home? . . . deodorant, maybe – or was it toothpaste? . . . what a memory – that's what comes of being overworked . . . I know, I'll send young Tom to London – if anyone's done a good job, it's that lad . . . yes, I'll slap his name down – which means I've got another memo to get out before the day's through . . . I wonder what Mary's up to – hope she's making the tea . . . is there anything else in this report I've got to action? . . . silly waste of time, half of it – I could've done the whole thing in a couple of pages . . . that's it – shampoo! I can get it when I go to lunch . . . wonder if Bob'll be in the pub today? . . . I could do with a pint right now . . . oh, Lord, now it's the telephone – never a minute's peace in this job . . .'

Since, thankfully, we are human beings and not machines, the wretched grasshopping bug can never be totally eradicated – but, if we are to do anything at all about managing time effectively, it *must* be controlled.

Flaming impatience

Look around you, and seek out those so-called managers (and others) who cannot distinguish between genuinely trying to save time and being downright impatient. People thus afflicted will nag and goad their way through each successive day, making life hell for those who are forced to work with them and under them. If anyone has the nerve to criticize such intolerance, the waspish response is usually to the effect that it's not impatience, but merely a desire for efficiency. In a pig's ear, it is . . . . Whichever way you look at it, impatience is the emotive stamp of the under-confident, the bored and the would-be tyrant; which must pose a question – which of these, if any, are you?

The 'tomorrow syndrome'

Aha, and here we have it! Next to laziness, procrastination is probably the most lousily infectious manifestation of GBMD in the book. Just savour the temptation: what can be more enticing than simply putting off until tomorrow what you don't feel like doing today? Think of all those marvellous get-out phrases:

'No, I'll need some peace and quiet for this one . . .'

'Tomorrow's another day . . .'

'I'll tackle it when I'm fresh . . .'

'No, John, I think I'd like to sleep on it . . .'

'It's not that urgent, anyway . . .'

'More haste, less speed – that's what I say . . .'

'This needs some thought . . .'

etc.

There is a world of difference between procrastination and the sensible allocation of priorities – how are you at self-delusion, Gunga Din?

Self-tutorial

Exercise 5

Arm yourself with a cup of coffee and, sitting back in that favourite chair, think objectively about your last day at work. No, a reflective overview is not enough – give detailed thought to each and every task you performed. To what extent was your efficiency marred by tumbling head-over-heels into the pitfalls of the Great British Management Disease? And, as you read these words, ask yourself: are you grasshopping right now?

Memory-prodder 4

It's time to gather the strings together with a reminder of what we've examined thus far; see Figure 1.

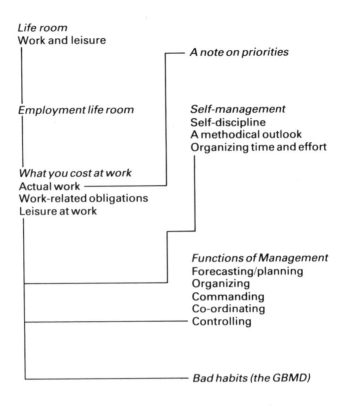

Figure 1   *Gathering the strings together*

More apropos of absolutely nothing

T'was in 1884 that an international conference agreed that the meridian passing through the Royal Observatory at Greenwich, London, should be the meridian from which other times in the world were calculated. Thus was born the base time, Greenwich Mean Time – but, Nature being what it is, even this varies due to changes in the speed of rotation of the Earth. To take account of this, time is now kept by atomic clocks (Co-ordinated Universal Time) and, in order that atomic and astronomical times are kept in step, the odd second is inserted or subtracted when necessary.

Of course, pub time is a different thing altogether.

5 Organizing and timing the bread-and-butter stuff

> Authors and uncaptured criminals . . . . are the only people free from routine.
>
> Eric Linklater,
> *Poet's Pub*

One dictionary's definition of a manager is: 'a person appointed alone or with others to conduct the working of, have effective control of, bend to one's will, cajole; find a way, contrive, be clever or stupid enough, bring about or secure . . . .' – and all that would seem to cover a multitude of sins, especially the 'be stupid enough' bit. Seriously, however (and, Lord save us, we must be serious), the definition fits hand-in-glove with Henri Fayol's good old original functions of management:'forecasting and planning, organizing, commanding, co-ordinating, and controlling' – and, whether we like it or not, leads us on to a simple, all-embracing conclusion.

A manager is a leader

Now, there's an earth-shaking truism for you but, remember, I'm being deadly serious, and it's time we asked ourselves a question. Just how much of a dedicated, effective leader can Mr Average-Joe Manager be when he's up to the armpits in the treacle of routine activities? The answer is, of course, there's no way in which any manager can be so immersed and, at the same time, keep his hands on the leadership reins. This is a crying shame, for one obvious reason:

All managers are saddled with routine duties

and one not-so-obvious reason:

Many managers positively love them, and won't put them down

Dear me, I can hear your anguished roar, 'Love routine duties? You must be joking – what on earth is attractive about doing the same old, boring tasks time and time again?' Well, all right, while I'm quite prepared to grant (at least, I think I am) that you are the exception to the general rule, the fact is that many managers rely on the repetitive, day-to-day stuff as the one and only cure for a number of executive itches and ills. By way of example, consider that most familiar of all routine chores, dealing with correspondence.

Those lovely, lovely letters

Ask any manager what he thinks of having to handle the twice-daily batch of letters, memos and the like, and the chances are you'll be treated to a heart-rending exposition on the evils of paperwork and, of course, the sheer back-breaking tedium involved. But, take my tip, ignore such tales of woe, and concentrate instead on the manner in which the selfsame story-teller keeps his executive claws firmly clenched on that which he professes to hate. The truth is, Mr Average-Joe Manager would die rather than let the task go to someone else – for, while he may believe what he hears, he won't be *satisfied* until he sees with his own eyes exactly what has been committed to paper:

> 'As you're probably aware, Clive, I'm what's known as a "self-made man", and I can tell you this for nothing – I see every bit of paper that comes and goes in my outfit. It's only by keeping tabs on the paperwork that I know exactly what's going on – and, believe you me, I need to know.'
> *Emphatic comment by the proprietor of an engineering firm, made while arguing the point at a management seminar.*

> 'Yes, I've got faith in my staff, but, well – I feel a jolly sight happier when I actually see the correspondence . . . I don't hog it, or anything like that, I just want to keep my finger on the pulse. I can't see anything wrong in that.'
> *Supporting observation by another manager at the same seminar.*

There are no two ways about it; a manager's lack of confidence in his staff, poor standards of self-discipline and, all too often, sheer curiosity and nosiness are the basic reasons for sticking like glue to this highly dubious tradition. Whatever *your* particular argument may be, why not carry out a slashing attack on the time you spend dealing with correspondence, and reap the benefits? Only last evening, Phil, one of the manager-students on a local IIM course, enlivened a fairly humdrum session with an extremely relevant contribution which, quoting from memory, ran thus:

> 'D'you know, the other day I realized for the first time that I'd got into this very habit of insisting on seeing every bit of paper in the department –

and, what's more, I realized why. As I've told you before, the boss had a custom of popping in and out of my office, asking all kinds of questions on this and that – and, because I was anxious to have all the answers, I made it my business to read every single thing going. Well, once again, he did his usual trick – but, this time, I just replied "Why don't you check with Bill Hughes, he's responsible for that?" He looked pretty surprised, so I capped it by saying "Look, we pay the man to be responsible for nothing but quality control – so, when you have a detailed query on that aspect, why not seek him out? That way, I don't have to speak from memory, with the risk that I give you duff information – you get the exact information, and I'm a bit more free to do the job you pay me for, managing." As I said, he looked a bit staggered at first, but then, would you believe it, he agreed with me one hundred per cent!'

At this point in Phil's account, some of the course members started burbling about 'passing the buck' and the evils of a boss being invited to sidestep his own manager – but our worthy manager-student quickly intervened:

'Hold on, the conversation didn't end there. I told my boss that, while I expected him to come to me with anything and everything concerning the policy or management of the department, there was absolutely no reason why he shouldn't address routine queries direct to the people concerned – and, again, he agreed. So, to cut a long story short, I now only read those bits of paper that my secretary decides I should read – and it's marvellous! Oh, yes, there's one more thing – I asked my boss why he was querying the obviously minor point on quality control, and d'you know what he said – "Oh, it was something I picked up when I was reading the mail." I tell you, we're all at it!

Phil was so right, we're all at it. Although the actual amount of time spent dealing with correspondence varies with the type of job and the ability of the manager concerned, the fact remains that we all tend to squander our meagre ration of hours and minutes carrying out what is, in reality, a paperwork over-kill. Conquer your doubts and inhibitions, and apply the drastic remedy:

a   Accept that your secretary or whoever you have selected to sort the mail, is good at her job (for why else would you have recruited her or him?). Have faith and give her the opportunity to prove her worth. Issue instructions that, with immediate effect, you only wish to see correspondence that actually demands your personal attention, *and nothing else* – and tell your secretary that she has the responsibility of absolute discretion in the matter.

b   Once you have carried out this brave step, grit your teeth and positively restrain yourself from constantly peeping over the girl's shoulder. Sure, it's likely that she'll commit some initial errors of judgement, but she'll soon learn – if, that is, you give her the chance.

c   Remember that the aching void in your self-confidence, that unsatiated urge to keep your finger on the pulse, can and should be assuaged by recourse to regular feedback and 'progress sessions' with the key members of your staff - but this does *not* mean popping in and out of your office like a Jack-in-the-box, feverishly checking that all is as it should be.

Okay then, let us assume that you've been sufficiently strong-willed to thus rid your in-tray of the correspondence dross – but what about the stuff that remains strictly your baby? Make use of the diagram in Figure 2 as food for thought and read the notes that follow.

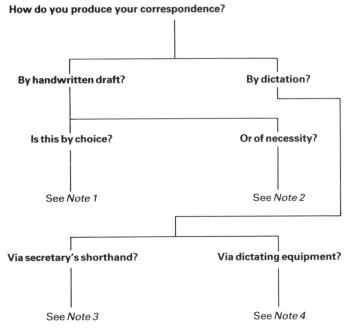

Figure 2   *Producing correspondence*

Note 1   You wretch. Here you are, dutifully ploughing through a book on the efficient management of time, when, in fact, you haven't even learned the basic adage about keeping a dog and barking yourself. So, what sterling reasons have you cooked up for electing to do drafts in longhand?

- It's a more precise method?
- Your secretary isn't really up to dictation?
- Ease of amendment?

If, as is probably the case, you have doubts about your ability to dictate correspondence (usually expressed as a 'dislike' of the game), it's high time you mastered this particular weakness. Face the problem head-on and, enlisting the help of your highly qualified secretary in the outer office, *get cracking*. Remember, up to now she will have had pretty jaundiced feelings about your refusal to use her talents – and she'll welcome a *volte-face*! If you need further encouragement to become a dictator (in the nicest sense of the word), remember also that your terrible habit of hand-writing drafts (at around 18 to 25 words per minute, compared with 100 to 130 words per minute for the spoken article) is dreadfully slow – and, hence, very expensive.

Note 2   The advent of new technology is certainly making its mark on the office scene, but there are still far too many managers who find themselves trying to cope in what amounts to a near Stone Age administrative ethos. If you are so cursed, all I can do is urge that you move heaven and earth to get things changed, and, of course, remind you of the quite startling cost-effectiveness, to say nothing of increased efficiency, inherent in a more modern approach – see Notes 3 and 4.

Note 3   Old habits die hard, and it may well be that you believe giving your secretary the chore of transcription from shorthand is the bee's knees in executive efficiency – but, truth to tell, it is not. Conversion to modern dictating equipment will increase the average secretary's transcription speed by 25 to 30 per cent – and, over a week, that's a hell of a lot of correspondence!

Note 4   Bully for you, you're sitting pretty! Or are you? Take a long, hard look at your dictating equipment. If it's over four or five years old, the likelihood is that it's well-nigh obsolete in terms of operational efficiency – *and* fully depreciated, to boot. Be with-it, wise and thrifty; find out how the new (and competitively priced) technology can save you hours of precious time and hence a good deal of money.

Having examined the alternative methods of producing paperwork, it's worth noting that, thus far, the only other thing I've hopefully achieved in this chapter is to persuade you to mercilessly prune your in-tray bumph and, by so doing, divert a pile of material on to the shoulders of your subordinates. This is all well and good but, if we're to treat this question of doing more in less time with any degree of realism, it's necessary to go a stage further and take a candid peep at, for want of a better term, your writing habits. And, since the proverbial sauce for the goose is sauce for the gander, what I have to say applies equally to all those members of staff who, clobbered or not with your correspondence fall-out, also have to write letters and memos.

The paperwork empire

Sadly, the foundations of any organization are built on the treacherous sands of paperwork – most of it bearing the stamp of verbosity and other composition ills, and much of it entirely superfluous. By far the worst aspect of a pretty grim picture is the dire proliferation of 'internal mail' – to wit, the interminable spawning by managers of that innocent sounding item, the memo. With utter self-candour, ask yourself the following questions:

1 Is it *absolutely necessary* to write a memo, or have you succumbed to the dreadful habit of automatically resorting to the beast?

2 Do you write memos because they provide, or so you think, splendid proof positive of your zeal and energy?

3 Do you ever remind yourself that a memo is an example of *one-way communication* and that, on more than the odd occasion, this could be the deep-down-under reason why you write them – an almost subconscious gambit to avoid direct confrontation?

As for your writing style, be it in memo, letter or other form – well, what *is* your writing style? Take a frankly appraising look at a representative sample of your most recent efforts, and measure them for their overall effectiveness:

1 To what extent are they sullied with hackneyed phrases and jargon?

72

'With reference to your . . .' *or* 'We acknowledge receipt of . . .'
instead of 'Thank you for . . .'

'. . . the contents of which are noted.'
instead of nothing at all – the phrase being entirely
superfluous.

'Enclosed please find . . .'
instead of I/We enclose . . .'

'. . . under separate cover . . .'
instead of '. . . separately . . .'

'Assuring you of our best attention at all times . . .'
YUK! The days of the Dickensian cringer are past, so why
be so determined to preserve them?

And so on.

2   To what extent does your written composition reflect those
    other, completely horrible aspects of the executive po-style:

    •   Ice-cold frigidity instead of friendliness – you know what I
        mean – the impersonal, as opposed to the personal
        approach?

    •   Everlasting attempts to impress by pomp, rather than by
        pleasant efficiency of manner?

So what on earth has one's writing style got to do with saving
time? The short answer is quite a lot. Lest you doubt this, think
of those nail-biting sessions when you either struggle with
handwritten drafts, or 'um' and 'er' your way through dictation.
One of the main reasons why managers find such work a positive
chore is because, quite simply and as I've already implied, *very
few of us tend to write as we speak* – every single sentence has to be
expressed in po-style, formal terms. This terrible compulsion not
only ensures that we produce a mass of written stuff which varies
in quality from the mediocre to the hideous, but also guarantees
that, in so doing, we gobble up great chunks of the working day.
Yes, indeed, one's writing style has a *great deal* to do with saving
time.

The 'information explosion' – and how to dodge the shrapnel

Tomorrow morning, when you stagger your secretary by instructing her to prune your current lion's share of the mail-bag, it's very likely that she'll come up with at least one burning question:

> 'So what about the other bits and pieces – the magazines, leaflets, brochures, and so on? What d'you want me to do with all those?'

There's no doubt about it, she will have a point – for, as you'll know to your cost, every post brings a ruddy avalanche of printed bumph of one sort or another. The trouble is, this places the manager in a classic, 'Catch-22' situation. On the one hand, he's constantly exhorted to keep with-it in terms of trends and developments in his work – and, on the other, he just hasn't got the time to cope with the sheer volume of reading that this entails. There are, shall we say, three alternatives:

1 *Preserve the good old status quo*   In a nutshell, continue to fumble through the daily pile, snatching a glance at this and that, placing the odd item on one side and heaving a regular half-ton straight into the waste-paper basket, unwanted and unread.

2 *Strive to be a sponge*   Step out on the short road to insanity by reading every single item – while, at the same time, trying to hold the job down.

3 *Or (remember?) adopt a methodical outlook*   Solve the problem by recourse to some very simple measures:
   - Decide exactly which items you wish to see in your in-tray, and inform your secretary accordingly – adding the proviso that she has absolute discretion in the case of the odd, out of the ordinary or important item.
   - Nominate various members of your staff to be responsible for reading *all* literature in specific areas; for instance, Bill White to cover office fittings and equipment, Jill Black to peruse everything on production, or whatever. Tell them your secretary will farm the material out and that you'll use the staff feedback sessions (which, of course, are a regular feature of the working week) to discuss anything they've found of value.

I'll leave it to you to decide which of the alternatives comes closest to satisfying the vital need to keep abreast of trends and developments –

and, just as important, is in full accord with the requirement to budget time and effort.

Hopefully, we're beginning to get organized . . .

Having dealt with two of the most vexing of all routine tasks – duties which, in aggregate, can soak up as much as two to three hours of an executive's working day – and having reminded ourselves once again that we're thinking in terms of *time and effort*, the point has been reached where we must put our finger on this chapter's crunch message. It is this: no matter what nature the routine task may take –

- Dealing with correspondence
- Surviving the information explosion
- Preparing figures, reports, returns, etc.
- Implementing regular inspections
- Checking progress on allocated tasks
- Setting up meetings, discussions, etc.

– the manager should not find it difficult to determine the order, analyse his method of approach, and schedule the time required for each such activity. The problems start when he tries to dovetail his carefully laid plans for actioning routine tasks with those other pitfalls in his daily round: people activities, 'thinking' and problem-solving. And, as I've already intimated, the next three chapters should scotch that little lot – if, that is, you've got the stamina and enough strong coffee to stay the course. What an infernal cheek – of course, you've got the stamina, for how else could you have possibly read thus far?

Self-tutorial

Exercise 6

None of us really enjoys having a rude finger poked at, of all things, our ability to write letters, memos, and so on – and I've just done exactly that. In an effort to prove me wrong, get someone with undoubted talent in the art to inspect a representative sample of your work. If all turns out to be well – why, accept my sincere apologies. If, er, things don't go quite as you expected – then, my friend, fly to the recommended reading list at the end of this book and you'll see that a man's gotta do what a man's gotta do . . .

Memory-prodder 5

You need only concern yourself with this memory-prodder if, indeed, you have progressed beyond the 'handwritten draft' stage and become a dictator of the to-be-written word. Think, with painfully candid recollection, of your last dictating session (to your secretary or into a machine, it matters little) and ask yourself the BIG QUESTION:

How good am I at dictation?

NO, by George, that's not what I meant! How dare you dismiss such an important point with a mere 'Fairly good' or 'About average'! Think again, thou miscreant manager.

- How many times do you say:

  'Um', 'Er', or what-have-you?

  'No, scrub that', 'Hold it – go back to the beginning', or similar verbal erasion?

- How guilty are you of:

  If relevant, failing to match your speed of dictation with your secretary's level of skill at taking it down?

  Failing to dictate punctuation marks, and *correct* ones, at that?

  Failing to spell awkward words, names, etc. without being asked?

  Walking up and down like a caged lion as you dictate?

  Tapping that pen on the desk, or indulging in some other and favourite fidget?

So ask yourself again:

How good am I at dictation?

More apropos of absolutely nothing

Some means of measuring time was found necessary even in the early days of civilization. The sundial, first mentioned in the Bible (II *Kings*, xx, 11) as the 'dial of Ahaz', is the oldest of timekeepers. It was succeeded, in about 300 BC, by the water clock – consisting of either a graduated bowl which sank in water by slow leakage, or a float which operated a pointer mechanically. Some 600 years later came the hour glass or sand glass which, nowadays, still takes pride of place when it comes to that three-minute egg. King Alfred's candle clock and the Japanese lamp clock recorded time by the consumption of the fuel feeding the wick. Mechanical clocks, driven by weights or springs, first made their appearance in about 1100 AD.

I'll swap my eight-digit calculator watch–chronograph alarm with hourly chime, solar cells, nightlight, 99-year calendar, melody player and all for a plain, simple ticker any time you like.

6 Organizing and timing the people bit

> The trouble with most managers is they can't tell the
> time.
>
> Anonymous

Many moons ago, I – and eleven other aspiring managers – had the
dubious privilege of sitting through a very expensive, inundated with
egg-heads course on leadership, which, although presented by one
of the country's leading 'colleges of management', ground slowly on
through four days of stultifying, bum-wriggling boredom. However,
on the morning of the fifth day, our lack-lustre, pickled-onion eyes
were greeted by the appearance of a new speaker at the rostrum, and,
before he'd uttered a word, we knew that things were about to
change – and, boy, were we right! Holding aloft one of the biggest
textbooks I've ever seen, the man pointed silently at the spine – and
then, waving his hand in a grandiloquent gesture of distaste, simply
let the tome drop to the floor with a resounding thump. There was a
second's startled pause before he spoke:

> 'Gentlemen, I trust you noted the title – *The Principles of Leadership*. If it
> takes nearly one thousand pages to explain the principles of leadership,
> how do you rate my chances of getting beneath the surface of the subject
> in forty minutes flat?'

He then proceeded to deliver a life-savingly splendid lecture, but
that's another story – for, by pinching the speaker's opening gambit,
I've made my point. Hundreds of books and millions of words (most
of them far too long and far too boring) have been written on the
subject of leadership – or, as the pundits are wont to term it, man
management. So, *caveat emptor*; if you expect this one measly chapter
to come up with earth-shaking philosophies-cum-recipes for
organizing and timing the 'people bit' of our executive lives, well, all I
can say is, you're in for a mighty big disappointment. For all the
titillating attractions, say, of 'transactional analysis' or any other much
publicized 'discovery', the hard fact is that there's nothing new under
the sun in this thing we call management, merely an army of people (I
nearly said con-men) who are expert in the art of putting new faces

and slants on age-old themes; and, of course, equally expert at inventing gobbledegook names to go with them. So here is one more angle on the vexed business of managing people more efficiently in less time – but, I hope, written in down-to-earth terms with a minimum of codswallop, and no wilful attempt to con.

All the successful managers I've ever come across have had one thing in common: each and every one has given the appearance of being totally unflustered and unworried. Yes, that's it, the efficient executive is the man or woman who, among other attributes, appears to others to have all the time in the world. There's a very good reason for this; instead of being squashed flat by the burden of the job, the good manager sits firmly on top of it. It's no illusion, they *do* have more time, simply because they've identified and either eradicated time-wasting factors, or learnt how to control them. Thus freed from bondage, these fortunate souls are able to give their undivided attention to the work which is rightly theirs, *managing* – and, magically, still find time to relax.

One such gifted man was Big Chief Sitting Bull, Red Indian equivalent of managing director to the Hunkpapa, Blackfoot and other Sioux tribes in the 1870s. Quick of thought and penetrating in judgement, Sitting Bull enjoyed a rare reputation for leadership and management counsel that extended far beyond his widespread Yellowstone and Missouri hunting grounds. Whether or not he was the first to utter those immortal words, 'no bad Injuns, only bad Chiefs', will never be known. What is certain is that, sitting impassively in his tepee, he orchestrated the mighty coalition that finally slew General George A. Custer, together with every officer and man in five companies, at Little Bighorn in 1876. In the eyes of Crazy Horse, Dirty Moccasins, Charcoal Bear and other chiefs, Sitting Bull had a vision (in these more enlightened days, we call it management perception) of victory over the white men who spoke with forked tongues – and, organizing his braves, sent them forth to achieve exactly that. Another certainty is that, like every successful manager since time began, Big Chief Sitting Bull got what he wanted by – you know what's coming – delegation.

Too right, there's no escaping this one

Since you're bound to know that delegation is the assignment of authority and responsibility to a subordinate for the carrying out of specific activities, I won't even mention it. But what I will ask is, how many of us actively remember that the function of an organization is to achieve its aims through planned, integrated endeavour – and that this can only be brought about with complete success if managers delegate correctly? It is only when an organization, be it a two-bit, hole-in-the-wall firm or a multi-national colossus, is blessed with managers who practise good delegation, so that all necessary tasks have been assigned, that the outfit stands firmly on the road to peak performance. However, and sadly, all this is wishful thinking – for the unpalatable truth is precious few managers do other than make a right dog's dinner of delegation.

Having tossed a generalized gauntlet at your feet, it's only fair that I give you the chance to shoot me down in flames – so here goes. See how you make out with yet another self-questionnaire, remembering, of course, that the usual rule applies – the truth, the whole truth, and nothing but the good old truth!

I tell myself I'm a delegator – but exactly how good am I at the game?

A Private note   Before I even look at the questions, I promise that I will not demean myself with flannel – if I'm to make any progress at all, I must heed that bit about the truth.

1   Do I *really* believe that delegation:
  - is a vital function of my role as a manager?
  - enables my subordinates to develop as individuals?
  - makes optimum use of their knowledge and experience?
  - releases me for more important tasks?

2   Or do I believe, wholly or partially, that delegation:
  - tends to undermine my authority?
  - prevents me from knowing fully what is going on?
  - is all very well for those managers with staff on whom they can rely?
  - doesn't really save me any time?

3   If I am in agreement with any of the points in Question 2, how do I feel about:
  - my authority as a manager? What is lacking in my make-up that causes me to feel such insecurity, and what am I doing about it?
  - the question of feedback from my staff? Do I make the effort

to ensure adequate discussion-cum-reporting – and if not, why not?

- the abilities and attitudes of my staff, and why am I content to merely cry in my beer instead of going all out for a remedy? Why don't I come to terms with the fact that *any* weakness or shortcoming in my subordinates is *my responsibility to correct?*

4 Getting to the nitty-gritty, do I ever think that delegation:
- just isn't worthwhile – because, with the time it takes to issue the instructions and answer all the blinking queries, I could do the job quicker myself?
- robs me of work that I know I can tackle (and which makes me look busy in the eyes of others), leaving me high, dry and exposed to the nasty aspects of my job?
- doesn't serve my aim to become *indispensable?*
- in these dangerous times, doesn't help me to *preserve my skin?*

In thus prompting you to grapple with your conscience, I have but one aim in mind: I want you to determine just how much of a *doer* you are at work, as opposed to *managing* things. Take a hard look at your average day and see, for instance, how it matches up to the appropriate ratios in Table 1.

Table 1 Time allocation guide

Level of management	Allocation of time	
	Proportion of time that should be spent on non-management activities	*Proportion of time that should be spent performing the role of management*
Managing director	10–15%	85–90%
Senior management	25–30%	70–75%
Middle management	45–50%	50–55%
Junior management	55–60%	40–45%
Supervisory grades	70–75%	25–30%

By the way, there is a super trap for the unwary in the percentages relating to 'middle' and 'junior' management levels – so, if either cap fits, do be warned! It is too easy for words, and a very convenient get-out, to swiftly glance at the figures, note their attractive approximation to 'half-and-half', and dismiss them airily with some such comment as 'Hum, around the fifty-fifty mark. Yes, I guess that's just about what I do, so I'm okay.' It's no jolly good, and well you know it! There is no alternative – you must place your daily round under stiff examination, uncover the maggots – and, in ruthlessly stamping on them, come up with the discovery that *efficient delegation really does save time.*

Giving those dratted instructions and passing information

One of a manager's biggest and most alarming failings is his very human inability to constantly audit and improve the manner in which he carries out the basic essentials of his job. And the deceptively dangerous business of giving instructions and passing information is a prime example of this particular Achilles heel. Be honest, when did you last question the general quality and content of your expressed wishes?

- For instance, are you in the habit of sporting a sergeant-major's badge on your executive sleeve, and issuing *commands* to all and sundry? No? Would your staff be inclined to agree with that vehement denial? What, I wonder, do they actually think of your choice of words, your tone – the very *timbre* of your holy edicts?
- Or, just perhaps, do you sadly try to get things done by coming out with utterances which, in tone and content, more closely resemble *pleas*? You know what I mean:
  'Sorry, Joe, but they're going to play merry hell upstairs if we don't come up with something soon – so would you like to . . .'

What is your 'personal style'? Now is the time to take stock of the situation and assess where you stand in the edict order of things:

Commands   If you happen to be on the barrack square, or you're around when a raging fire breaks out in the office, then, by all means, resort to commands. Otherwise, *don't.*

Instructions, requests and suggestions   Plainly, these are the vehicles a manager should utilize when making his wishes known – but, if he is to succeed in terms of saving time (to say nothing of preserving good working relationships), he must select with care:

'John, bring me the file on Brownlow, please.'

'John, would you get me the file on Brownlow, please?'

'John, it'd probably help if you looked out the Brownlow file.'

Pleas Well, if you're a management worm you will continue to plead your way through life, whatever I say.

However, the art of getting people to carry out one's wishes at work goes an important stage further than the mere selection of words and tone. If time is to be properly saved in the long run, a modicum of the precious commodity must be expended at the outset in ensuring that each and every instruction, request or suggestion contains four vital elements:

- An explanation **why** the action is necessary – making clear the aims and objectives.

- Full details of **how** it is to be achieved, and the allocation of adequate authority and responsibility (in simple terms, the power required to perform the task and due accountability for its completion).

- The **motivation** of whoever is concerned to give of his or her best by ensuring, among other things, that the subordinate is fully in the picture about what has to be done. In short, fuelling that fire in the belly.

- An opportunity for **discussion** and **suggestion** – let the poor sap who's been clobbered with the task put in his or her (often very valuable) oar. Is it false pride that prevents us from acknowledging that, nine times out of ten, our subordinates beat us hands-down in spotting snags and short cuts?

And what of disseminating information in general? Are you one of those managers who, sitting in a perfectly normal, run-of-the-mill post, tends to regard the simple process of opening his mouth as a threat to national security? The caution principle is all fine and dandy for the managers who ply their wares under the prohibitive cloak of the Official Secrets Act, but the odds are that you're not one of them – so get out there and tell your people what is happening, and what is likely to happen. The regular and succinct dissemination of information tends, once again, to save time in the long run – and involves those who are entitled to be involved.

The neglected art of counselling

Counselling is not, as is popularly supposed, a process to be brought out of the executive cupboard on such hopefully rare occasions as an all out strike. No, very far from being an emergency procedure, *the objectives of counselling are to improve employees' performance, efficiency and personal effectiveness.* The manager who ignores counselling until such time as the stark facts of a situation force him into action is a time-wasting idiot, totally unfit for his role as a leader and director of people. However small an outfit may be, its overall efficiency and harmony of function depend on regular two-way communication, and counselling represents an ideal opportunity to practise exactly that.

I know of one very able manager who reserves a good part of his Monday morning routine for counselling – although, being wise, he refers to the get-togethers as 'chat sessions', thereby removing the palpable taint of formality. He tells me, and I believe him, that this regular activity enables him to implement and consolidate a number of essential executive functions:

- Allocating tasks – the delegation bit.
- Receiving and reviewing reports on progress – giving due regard to that important business of 'accountability'.
- Giving information – keeping his subordinates in the picture.
- Seeking suggestions 'from those who know' (his words) on ways and means of improving efficiency.
- Nipping grievances in the bud 'before they blossom into crises' (again, his words).
- Dealing informally with matters of petty discipline and hiccups in what he terms his 'organization climate'.
- And, of course, giving his full attention to those odd times when staff welfare problems rear their urgent heads.

Like everything else, if employee counselling is to be a successful, time-effective process, it must be conducted along logical lines. Yes, by all means, call them chat sessions to encourage participation, but never, ever, allow them to actually degenerate into casual, gossipy conversations – for, if you're anything like human, there's far too much of that already, and one object of the vital exercise is to *save* time, not squander more of it. There is a handy recipe for counselling success:

- *The break-ice routine*   A brief, amicable and efficient 'steer-round' to the topics for discussion. And, dare I say it, the manager who envisages difficulty with this ice-breaking process is the manager with a dangerous weakness – so think on't.

- *Taking, and keeping, the reins*   The counselling interview may be an informal process, but the wise manager will, nevertheless, ensure that it is always a friendly, steered discussion.

- *Listening properly*   Have you observed how some misguided and rude people 'listen' when others are speaking – they look everywhere but at the speaker, fidget, steal glances at their wristwatch, interrupt, and so on? Are you one such 'listener'? Enough said!

- *Watching for tell-tale signs*   The good counsellor will be on the alert for signs of nervousness, hesitation, irritation, fear of losing face and umpteen other symptomatic give-aways in the subject's face, attitude and comments. Watch those eyes, for they can tell a fulsome story.

- *Asking the right questions*   Those good old open-ended questions are the ones that produce information – so use them:
  Why was that?
  How did that come about?
  What happened then?
  etc.

Oh, yes, indeed, employee counselling is a vital adjunct to good management in general, and the efficient handling of time in particular. Clasp your resolution in both hands, and give it a really good try.

Handling the greatest time-waster of them all

And what might that be? Why, *meetings*, of course! Nothing, but nothing, weighs down the management yoke more than the horrifically subjective, interminably time-consuming and, it seems, unavoidable get-togethers that masquerade under the umbrella of that innocuous little word, meetings. Approaching the subject with my usual delicacy of touch, let me say straight away: you show me a manager who enjoys meetings, and I'll show you an executive hobgoblin who uses them as a magnificent excuse to be away from his desk and his real responsibilities. Cruel words, or a stark home-truth? I'll leave you to judge – and, in the meantime, offer some tips (none of them original, you understand – how on earth could they be?) for use on those awful occasions when *you* are fated to chair a meeting.

- *Do your homework*   Always study the purpose of the meeting and, if there is one, the agenda. Beware of that jabberwock of the organization everglades, the informal meeting – when adequate preparation is a prerequisite for time-saving survival.

- *Show that you mean business, time-wise*   Once seated on the throne, remove your wristwatch and place it where you, and everyone else, can see it – bang-smack on the table in front of you. And never forget its telling message.

- *Clarify what is afoot*   As the session hopefully progresses from point to point, ensure that all the participants (even old Jim in the corner) know exactly what is going on. You can bet your life that someone will be in the dark, albeit through lack of attention.

- *Ensure full participation*   To put it in a nutshell, gag the garrulous and encourage the shy or otherwise unforthcoming to contribute. Incidentally, for goodness sake keep the discussion on course – remembering that one of the biggest problems in ensuring adequate participation is preventing all and sundry from careering off on time-gobbling tangents.

- *Summarize regularly*   Each topic and decision should be summarized – not only for the benefit of the participants, but also to enable the hapless minute-taker to make some sense of the proceedings!

- *If you are the chairman, act like one*   Steer the thing or it'll run away with you. There is nothing quite so tragic as a chairman clinging frantically to the neck of a bolting horse!

- *Obtain agreement*   For, of course, that's what a chairman's job is all about – obtaining a consensus. Whenever it is humanly possible, do so.

- *Behave yourself!*   Contrary to the obvious beliefs of many mismanagers, the business of chairing a meeting is not to be regarded as an opportunity to flaunt one's self-importance – or, for that matter, as a licence to practise any other nasty habits. A firm, friendly and impartial chairman will rapidly gain the respect of any meeting – and, although he may not realize it, will have Old Father Time battling on his side.

Plainly, the boss who wishes to conduct efficient and productive meetings with his subordinates has to make a fairly knotty decision: namely whether or not the sessions should be conducted formally or informally. One thing is certain, whatever his decision, the style and tenor of the meetings will have a profound effect on his staff as a whole and will set the tone for the regard in which he is held by each and every member of the team. With this sombre *caveat* in mind, it is wise to remember that while meetings conducted along rigidly formal lines may save time, they run the risk of inhibiting those who participate in them – and, believe you me, such frustrated communication can sound the death-knell for efficient management in no time flat. A degree of formality is necessary, if only to combat the inevitable gibble-gabble of completely casual affairs, but the wise, time-conscious manager will set his sights on a happy compromise – meetings in which close relationships founded on mutual respect ensure maximum participation by all concerned. Given such an ambience and a boss who knows his chairmanship ropes, why, then the meeting is no longer the biggest time-waster of them all, it becomes what it should have been all along, an essential and highly viable tool of management.

Think hard about organizing and timing the all-important people bit, and if the process of exercising the good old grey matter causes you any concern, never fear – for that's what the next chapter is about!

Self-tutorial

Exercise 7

Here's a nice, cosy little task for you: an armchair exercise involving just a little thought on – you've got it in one – delegation. Simply take a look at the following tasks and decide which ones should be delegated. Yes I know that personal circumstances dictate events, and there is a whole heap if 'ifs' and 'buts' inherent in this type of thing, with the result that you're hardly likely to agree with what, perforce, is a pretty academic exercise. But, for all that, have a go. Compare your answers with those provided at the end; and, in expressing your disdain, you'll be doing exactly what I want you to do – *thinking about delegation*.

1   Making your appointments and maintaining your appointments diary.

2   Drafting office or other procedural instructions which affect your bailiwick.

3   Opening mail marked 'Personal and Confidential', addressed to you by name.

4   Compiling an appraisal report on a member of your staff.

5   Approving expenditure on office stationery.

6   Deciding on the establishment of a new post within your department.

7   Dealing with visiting representatives.

8   Formulating your departmental budget.

Okay, let's see just how widely we disagree. However, do bear in mind that the value of the exercise as a whole is directly proportional to your degree of personal candour. Do not, I beg, say to yourself, 'I already do so-and-so this or that way – so, subject closed'! Look keenly at existing arrangements – would a visiting, recognized expert agree with your methods? *Think delegation*.

1   If you have a secretary, then allow her (or him) to be one in every sense of the word. Delegate the task of making your appointments and keeping your diary – you tell her when you will not be available, and she'll tell you when you've got to be! Any doubts you may have on this task reflect directly on you; after all, you selected your secretary, so if she isn't up to it, it's your fault – but, be honest, isn't it more probably the case that you just don't want to relinquish the reins?

2   If you have a supervisor or other senior employee, then delegate the task of *initially* drafting such instructions, for this subordinate is almost certain to be more closely associated than you'll ever be with the nitty-gritty detail involved and he or she *needs* the experience. Your rightful task is to discuss,

amend and approve the produce of your subordinate's labour.

3   There's no doubt about it, this business of personal and confidential mail is a thorny subject. Everything, of course, depends on the relationship you have with your secretary and, dare I say it, the type of mail you are likely to receive. However, the sad fact remains that too many really proficient secretaries are starved of full responsibility and trust by unthinking bosses, and the whole object of this particular item is to pose the question: are *you* such a boss?

4   If the appraisal scheme concerned demands personal completion by the manager, then, clearly, the task cannot be delegated. However, I'm pretty sure you'll agree that the employee's supervisor, if there is one, should certainly be consulted and, infinitely better, invited to complete a pen-picture of the employee's performance. Once again, in addition to helping you, this will provide the supervisor with valuable experience, and that's what delegation is all about.

5   With some organizations, when it comes to spending lolly the process of delegation is regarded as little short of madness, positively inviting financial and criminal disaster. If you are unlucky enough to work within such an outfit, your task is clear – get in there and fight like fury for the right to delegate such mundane tasks as routine, minor expenditure, not forgetting that your job as manager will involve the duty of checking and auditing (which does *not* mean sitting on people's shoulders).

6   Deciding on the creation of a new post is definitely a management function. Quite obviously, consultation is involved – *isn't it?*

7   If, as I hope is the case, you have delegated the task of examining all that trade literature to selected subordinates, then, for crying out loud, give those very same people the job of dealing with the regular flood of visiting representatives. And, since you have pride in your organization (for why else would you stay?), ensure that each and every rep is afforded a modicum of courtesy – not a peremptorily rude brush-off, as is so often the case.

8   We all know the essential difference between 'formulating' and 'finalizing', or do we? Let your subordinates utilize their abilities in having an initial stab at producing appropriate sections of budgets

etc. Then, following consultation, you can do your own bit and, with a flourish of trumpets, produce the final *tour-de-force*.

Yes, think delegation – and remember, it does save time

Memory-prodder 6

Effective and regular employee counselling produces marked improvements in subordinates' morale and personal efficiency – and, as a consequence, saves valuable time. In sticking like glue to the five principles of good counselling –

1 Breaking the ice
2 Steering the session
3 Listening hard
4 Asking the right questions
5 Watching for tell-tale signs

– the manager cannot avoid achieving these vital objectives.

Watching for tell-tale signs
Nervousness, hesitation, gestures, facial expressions, the look in the eyes, etc., may be evidence of:

Inadequate training or experience
Insecurity in the job
Insecurity as a member of the work group
Out-of-work personal problems
A management fall-down (insufficient guidance, etc.)
Fear of change
Over-confidence
Fear of losing face

More apropos of absolutely nothing

As is well known, the phenomenon of 'jet lag' is now recognized as a good reason for globe-trotting executives to postpone any important business for at least twelve hours after completion of a long flight. As is also well known, there are many in the ranks of management who assiduously apply the same principle to their forty-minute commuting stints, ignoring the fact that their early morning inertia is caused by body-clocks with weak mainsprings. Stop blaming the 8.15 from Penge, and get with it.

7 Come to think of it . . .

BRAIN, *noun.* An apparatus with which we think that we think.

Ambrose Bierce,
The Devil's Dictionary

I don't know about you but one of my pet hates is the apparent ease with which so many of our so-called 'authorities' on management lay down grandiose principles of executive behaviour and, in so doing, blithely ignore the fact that we poor damned managers are only human, after all. For example, a treatise on the art of thinking may well kick off with the exhortation, 'To be of any value thinking must be constructive and, above all, purposeful.', and, having planted this pearl of wisdom, will immediately proceed to bigger and more erudite things – without a single mention of all the mental wrinkles that, given a month of Sundays, will still prevent the average manager from surmounting this first, vital fence. Forgive my labouring the point, but, for goodness sake, you and I already know that thinking must be 'constructive and purposeful'; surely, what we want to be told is *how* to set about it? Well, justified moan or not, let's have a bash at exactly that!

For starters, place your hand on the back of your head and, as it rests there, just think . . . Directly beneath your palm, cushioned and protected by Nature's magnificent nut-case, is the ever-ticking, cerebral cortex region of your brain. Containing over 90 per cent of your share of nerve cells, this mental operations room is tasked with the reception and interpretation of countless sensory impulses. The largely unmapped areas of the cortex are believed to be concerned with memory, intelligence and imagination – those magical human attributes that set us apart from the common herd. It is here, beneath your hand, that you are thinking about what is beneath your hand, and it is the working of this wondrous cerebral grey matter which we must now examine.

There are three fuelling processes on which our individual 'thinking engines' depend, and, if you like, it is the quality of each of these fuels which, in sum, determines our mental performance:

Gut-feelings

Education and experience

Comprehension

Gut-feelings

More properly known as instinct (but, as you should have realized by
now, I have a yen for the improper), gut-feelings can be the friend or
deadly foe of mankind – depending, of course, on whether they turn
out to be right or wrong. A great deal of our thinking is conditioned
by their Siren-like attraction, and I dare say we can all recall instances
when, despite having been faced with a clearly logical course of
action, a gut-feeling has impelled us in the opposite, illogical
direction. One classic example of this weakness is the student-pilot
who, finding himself flying in cloud, chooses to rely on his gut-
feeling that the aircraft is straight and level – when, in fact, his
instruments tell him it is not. Seconds later, he ends up as a messy
blot on the landscape. Another fine example which is much closer to
home is our unfailing propensity to gut-feelings in the field of
selection, most aptly summarized by those immortal words 'I know a
good chap when I see one.'

So, how the devil can we aspire to constructive and purposeful
thought when, whether we like it or not, we are constantly at the
mercy of gut-feelings? The short answer is that they must be
recognized for what they are – often illogical, always intensely
subjective, and *highly dangerous* gambles. One effective measure is
the adoption of a rock-hard mental resolution:

> 'I will always ask myself the question: to what extent is my line of thought
> supported by the *facts* of the situation – or am I merely prey to a pure and
> simple gut-feeling?'

Education and experience

The second fuelling process in this funny old business of thinking is
our constant mental resort to past education and experience. From,
say, potty-training onwards, we *learn* as we trek through life,
sometimes with comfortable ease but, more often than not, the hard
way. Buried deep in that cerebral cortex is an infinitely elastic data
bank which constitutes the storehouse of such accrued knowledge,
and in which we tend to scrabble. I use the term 'scrabble' with good

reason – for, when faced with the need to think, many of us fail to make *relevant* demands on our data bank and, as a result, the process is doomed from the start. In drawing on past education and experience, it is the wise person who will ask himself:

'Is this stuff *relevant* to the matter in hand?'

'Is it *fact* or *assumption?*'

Comprehension

The third and crunch process on which constructive and purposeful thinking depends is the ability to comprehend and deduct, or to mentally proceed from the general to the particular – in short, and with due exercise of those brain cells, to come up with a well-defined and logical conclusion. The marvellous thing about comprehension is that it not only enables us to cope with life and steer clear of trouble, it is also the very means by which we revamp and increase our accrued knowledge and experience.

All right then, let us take a look at an example of the three aspects of thinking in action. Imagine, if you will, that the manager, John, is getting himself into a mental brew over Joe, a recalcitrant and increasingly disruptive employee. Having thus minimally set the scene, it is now necessary for us to climb inside John's head – see Figure 3.

And, yes, we can all guess the likely outcome of that little fairy tale – and picture the scene as poor old John wriggles painfully on the hot-seat of the tribunal witness stand. Be that as it may, my example has taken us within a hair's breadth of problem-solving, and that is due for an examination in the next chapter – so, back to 'thinking in general'.

Routine, regular and VITAL thinking

Although pretty obvious, it's worth noting that it is the degree to which a manager is capable of thinking constructively and developing new ideas that, by and large, will determine his success or failure as a boss. While many executives profess to using the time spent in commuting to and from work for good, solid thought, constructive thinking really must be planned as an integral part of the work routine. It is part and parcel of the manager's job to make

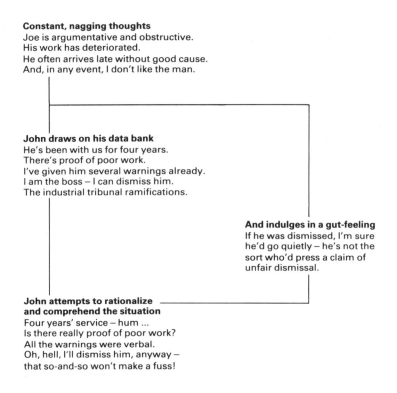

Constant, nagging thoughts
Joe is argumentative and obstructive.
His work has deteriorated.
He often arrives late without good cause.
And, in any event, I don't like the man.

John draws on his data bank
He's been with us for four years.
There's proof of poor work.
I've given him several warnings already.
I am the boss – I can dismiss him.
The industrial tribunal ramifications.

And indulges in a gut-feeling
If he was dismissed, I'm sure
he'd go quietly – he's not the
sort who'd press a claim of
unfair dismissal.

**John attempts to rationalize
and comprehend the situation**
Four years' service – hum ...
Is there really proof of poor work?
All the warnings were verbal.
Oh, hell, I'll dismiss him, anyway –
that so-and-so won't make a fuss!

Figure 3   *An example of thinking in action*

adequate time for it, and it will be time well spent.

However, be warned; it is simply no use restricting one's planning to the inclusion of 'think sessions' in the daily round, in the pious hope that when the moment arrives, one's mind will be inundated with beautifully constructive thoughts – would that it did work like that, but no way! Once time has been allocated, the manager must list his specific areas of responsibility and *then* think constructively of ways and means to bring about improvements in each of them, one after another. Here is a sample list, with some likely 'triggers' for your consideration:

People

a   Exactly what is the state of the organizational climate within my bailiwick?
b   If adverse in any way, what am I doing about improving morale? *Remember*, your detached 'overview' of morale may be vastly different from that which actually pertains. The big question is how do your staff view the situation?

96

c Is the existing distribution of work stretching the abilities of *every* member of my staff, or is there room for improvement?

d When did I last review job specifications, and to what extent have my people's duties 'drifted and changed' since then? Or, if the cap fits, *why* have I never carried out such a review?

e Staff development and training?

Methods

a When did I last review the efficacy of methods in use, both administrative and technical?

b Am I completely satisfied that all our methods and procedures still serve the purpose for which they were originally designed, and that we are not harbouring outmoded or unnecessary practices in our midst?

Planning

a Like it or not and whatever my status, one of my duties is to plan for the future. There is no way round this obligation. I *must* forecast and lay plans in terms of:

Increasing output/sales
Gaining new customers
Increasing our capacity
Reducing costs
Reviewing prices
Reviewing my part of the organization
New products activities

So, gathering the strings together, what have we got up to now? We've considered the three primary components of the thinking process, and blithely emphasized the need for the manager to indulge in regular periods of constructive and purposeful thought. Is that the end of the battle – are we now ready and equipped to become efficient thinking machines at the drop of a hat? Sorry about this, but the answer is a resounding 'NO'!

It may seem a rather convoluted request, but just think about thinking. Plainly, it is this lifelong, unceasing mental process that triggers and governs our every activity, but there are umpteen occasions when we sit back with the physical gear literally in neutral, and engage ourselves in thought – and thought alone. Now, if this is true, if we have developed the almost reflex habit of sliding happily into the 'thinking mode', and if, by so doing, we have coped successfully with all that has come our way, why on earth is it necessary to devote this entire chapter to something we've been doing since we were born, and doing pretty well? The truth is, in terms of the efficient use of time (to say nothing of the knotty business of achieving a logicality of thought), we *don't* do it very well. Day-dreaming is one thing, solid thinking is quite another. There are a number of pitfalls inherent in the latter which most of us fail to avoid:

- *Solitude* In Biblical times, certain worthies took to the nearest convenient wilderness when faced with the need to think, thereby obeying a rule that holds good to this very day: namely, that solitude aids thought. Unfortunately, the turmoil and incessant hubbub of modern life is such that, even if we manage to achieve solitude (and it's becoming quite a task), many of us experience actual discomfort at being thus 'cut off' from our fellows. Just as today's teenager often requires the background bawl of a transistor radio for nothing more than company, his adult counterpart has come to depend on the presence and noise of others for heart's ease. Ah, yes, there may be vehement protestations along the lines of 'I want to be alone' and all that jazz, but when it comes to the crunch, relatively few of us actually *enjoy* solitude for very long. To be more precise, we've forgotten the marvellous art of self-sufficiency, and the consequent 'vacuum' of solitude becomes for many an almost intolerable burden. All of which is bad news for innumerable would-be thinkers.

- *Interruptions* If we don't go for the solitude bit (and closing the office door may not be included under that heading), it's a fair bet that we'll be assailed with that grizzly concomitant of today's hubbub, interruptions – and we all know what happens to serious thought when Uncle Tom Cobley and the rest of the tribe keep butting in. There's a postscript to this one: having said that closing the office door cannot be regarded as genuine 'solitude', with some of us the act is sufficient to make us feel horribly alone – to the point where we actually welcome interruptions! Once again, the process of thinking isn't exactly helped by this weakness.

- *Lack of self-confidence* A weak dose of faith in one's own abilities is a sure-fire step on the road to defeat in any theatre of human activity, especially thinking. And the manager who constantly worries about the opinions others may have of his skills and capabilities is similarly doomed to failure. In both cases, throwing a dice would be far more effective than trying to think.

- *Cheating*   Pinching other people's ideas is an act of piracy which is not only reprehensible, but very dangerous to boot. The inimitable Sod's Law makes special provision for those who commit such larceny: 'He who purloins the efforts of his fellow man shall suffer unexpected disaster at the worst possible moment.' But the warning is probably a sheer waste of time – for, as I've queried elsewhere in these chapters, would such a scallywag be bothering to read this book?

- *Self-delusion*   One of the most tempting ways to pass up a thinking task is to swiftly delude oneself that, in fact, there is really no necessity for it; that to engage in the process would be making a mountain out of a molehill, thus wasting valuable time. Actually, this weakness is merely a more artful version of the next one in the list.

- *Downright laziness*   Not, you understand, the straightforward rejection of a thinking session from the outset (although, crikey, that's bad enough), but, rather, the heinous business of making all the preparations, usually with an impressive flourish of trumpets – and then doing precisely nothing. I'm reminded of bygone days when, as a thoroughly rotten and pimply adolescent, I was faced with the job of revising for school exams. Ah yes, I'd make a great show of digging out textbooks, telling all and sundry about the magnitude of the task – and then, with hand on brow, repair to my bedroom, where I'd do precisely nothing. There are those managers who put on an exactly similar show at work, little realizing that everyone, particularly their subordinates, can see through their little act. How often does the *mañana* syndrome embrace *you* in its clammy grasp?

And so on, *ad infinitum*. Why not add to the list by thinking about your own, very individual 'thinking pitfalls' – and, as you do so, try to avoid the ones I've listed?

Self-tutorial

Exercise 8

As we progress through these pages, we are gradually approaching the stage where, instead of dealing with the question of efficient time management in very general terms, we will be having a stab at quantifying and apportioning the brute. This exercise is intended to take us a few steps nearer that goal, simply by prompting you to adopt a more objective regard for the utilization of time spent in thought.

Firstly, it is necessary for you to select a subject. Let's say a 'people' or 'methods' topic – something from the work scene that not only bears thinking about, but will also produce dividends. Yes, I know, it's difficult to think of something off the cuff but, if you're really stuck, why not review your last day's stint in the office, and select the subject that gave you most pause for thought? It doesn't matter if you reached a conclusion – for the purpose of this exercise, re-think the thing through.

Having selected your subject, and before you dutifully career off on a flood-tide of generalized thought, grit your teeth and force yourself to fall in line with the following *modus operandi*:

- Attain *solitude and silence* to enable you to think clearly.

- Having recognized your subject, mentally review and amass all the *relevant* information.

- A proportion of this information will be *fact*, some will consist of personal opinion derived from your accrued knowledge and experience, and some will be pure and simple *gut-feeling*. The next and essential step is to apportion the information under these three headings, and eliminate every vestige of gut-feeling from your mind. What's that, easier said than done? Yes – *but do it.*

- Refrain from flippancy of thought. Consider each thought or idea with the care that such fragile things deserve.

- Beware of preserving the *status quo* as a lazy or cowardly alternative to innovative thought.

- Do not allow wishful thinking to become an active ingredient in your thought processes.

- If relevant, afford the known opinions of others a decent mental hearing, accepting or rejecting them on logical (not emotive or imagined) grounds.

As they say in the US Navy, now hear this: *go no further than the end of this paragraph*. Having read the foregoing, did you carry out my request and actually pick a subject for thought? If, as is most likely the case, you didn't, now is the time to redeem yourself. Go on, be a brave, hard-working soul – select a topic and give it the treatment.

Okay, I'll accept your assurance that you've completed a period of logical and deductive thought; but roughly how long did it take to thus exercise your mind? Seconds – minutes? How many minutes do you think? And, of that guestimated period, what proportion of *your time* was wasted in fruitless and illogical mental meandering? Get the message?

Memory-prodder 7

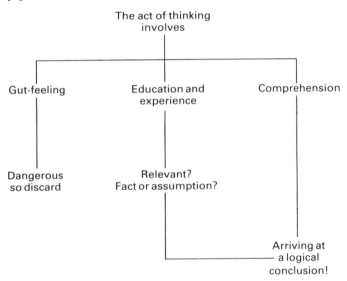

Figure 4   *The act of thinking*

More apropos of absolutely nothing

The 'biological clock' is something more than the cause of inconvenient complications when you and I cross man-made time zones. It is the infernal device seated deep within ourselves that spawns and perpetuates habitual expectations and requirements – and the habit of expecting and requiring breakfast at 'breakfast time' is merely one manifestation of it. Here's a salutory thought for your digestion: when, and to what extent, does your biological clock control your mentally 'switched-off' periods?

Before you resort to the easy get-out 'Oh, quite obviously, when I'm at home watching the goggle-box', think about it a bit more. Are there other occasions in the day when you habitually wind down – say, during working hours? And have you got into the habit of styling such very pleasant switched-off periods as 'thinking time'?

8 Hold on, there's a wee problem

It isn't that they can't see the solution. It is that they can't see the problem.

G.K. Chesterton,
The Scandal of Father Brown

One particularly plaintive cry from the heart to be heard in many a college staff-room is 'This lecturing business would be a cracking good job if it weren't for the students.' I guess there are many battle-scarred executives who would similarly offer that management would be a good job, if it weren't for the problems. But, life being what it is, college lecturers are paid to suffer students, and no amount of crying in one's beer will alter the fact that managers are paid to solve problems. Mind you, in some countries (but not, as we all know, in the United Kingdom) managers receive *top* salaries for their day-to-day dealings with awkward people and knotty situations. But, again as we all know, we don't sweat blood merely for the privilege of earning filthy lucre, do we – it's the pure joy of the game that keeps us coming back for more . . . Ah well, having done my small bit for the cause, let's see if we can give the vexed business of problem-solving a time-conscious kick-around.

If we assume, just for a wee, unrealistic moment, that a manager is nothing more than a machine, it is simplicity itself to express problem-solving as a sub-system of his mechanism: see Figure 5.

But, despite some opinions to the contrary, a manager is not a machine, he is a mere human being, beset with frailties – and I, for

Figure 5   *The machine-manager as problem-solver*

one, am very glad he is. However, there's no escaping the fact that his weaknesses bring considerable complications in their wake, and this is particularly evident when it comes to solving problems. With his human propensities in mind, any attempt to produce a nice, clear-cut systems diagram is now a slightly hairy proposition; see Figure 6.

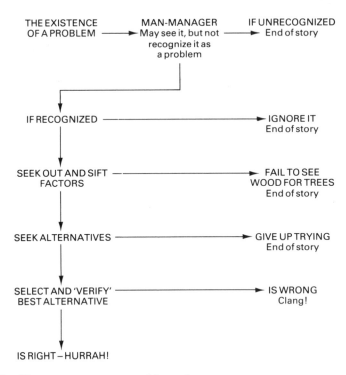

Figure 6   *The man-manager as problem-solver*

And that little lot is the simplified version . . .

If we are to come anywhere near producing a time-saving survival kit for problem-solving, it is necessary to gather together the vital component actions involved – remembering that, in the real, workaday world, to omit even one would be to court almost certain disaster.

Problem-solving in six difficult steps

Step 1   Recognizing that a problem exists and clearly identifying it

I once had the worrying privilege of serving under a boss who, even if faced with the terror and finality of Armageddon, would probably fail to acknowledge the existence of even a teeny-weeny problem in his complacent scheme of things. Endowed (or should it be cursed?) with the artlessness of a saint, he burbled his way through working life and, by his utter inability to recognize problems, created virtual mayhem at every juncture. Since little can be done to help such way-out individuals, except, perhaps, stamp them out of existence, it is more realistic to turn our attention to the positive horde of managers who know problems exist – but, try as they might, cannot identify them clearly and concisely.

Consider, if you will, the classic example of the guy who, prone to this weakness, finds himself facing the dire emergency of a fire at work. His instinctive reaction to such a non-routine occurrence might well be to identify the fire as a 'single problem' and, thus triggered, rush around dividing his energies between efforts at fighting the blaze, warning and seeing staff to safety, saving essential documents, and so on. On the other hand, a manager not prone to the weakness might well identify *two* problems, fighting the fire and getting people out of the building – and, armed with his acuity of perception, decide that the latter problem required his undivided, priority attention.

It is the non-routine problems that create difficulties of identification. When they crop up, the wise manager will always ask himself the same question:

'Is this the *real* problem *or*:
    a product of it?
    a combination of problems, requiring allocation of priorities?'

Step 2   Gleaning the facts

To be more explicit, separating the factual wheat from the chaff. I do not intend to insult your intelligence by subjecting you to a lengthy paragraph on the paramount need to gather all the relevant facts, for you're already aware of this salient requirement. But I do deem it necessary and relevant to emphasize the bit about the chaff! Facts are one thing, *assumptions* are quite another – so, before making them, ask yourself:

'What are my *grounds* for assuming thus?'

'To what extent are these grounds supported in *logic?*'

Step 3   Pinpointing the cause of the problem

Having established the existence and relevant facts of a problem, we seem to have an in-built tendency to plunge straight into the business of solving it without bothering to establish the *cause* – probably because it's often difficult to do exactly that. But it is also difficult to solve the crux of a problem until the cause *is* pinpointed, so in the interests of time-saving efficiency, whenever possible, it must be done.

To illustrate the importance of this stage in the problem-solving process, imagine that Tom, your office supervisor, has recently become a father. Known to you for some time as a hard-working, unflappable and kindly individual who is respected and liked by his juniors, you are perturbed by the fact that, since the birth of his son, Tom has undergone a distinct change of temperament. Now lacking in concentration, he has become little short of irascible in his dealings with the staff and, in short, is the very antithesis of his former self. Not unnaturally, you decide that the situation must be resolved, and you have him in for what you hope will be a full and frank discussion about his current, strangely uncharacteristic behaviour. Initially, to your surprise and disappointment, things prove abortive in that Tom is irritably reluctant to even talk about his troubles. However, you persevere and, prompted by your careful handling of the session, it emerges that the birth of his son does, indeed, have much relevance where his change in temperament is concerned. Persevering still further, and taking great pains over your own attitude in what is proving to be a most critical counselling session, you finally win Tom over – and are somewhat shattered when he blurts out the tragic fact that his baby son was born with physical deformities.

The object of this hopefully rare but entirely possible story is not only to remind you of the vital need to establish the real cause of any problem, but, also, to illustrate how a failure to do so can, and nearly always will, seriously affect any solution. In the case of Tom, if it was a real-life situation, I'd like to think that the root cause of the problem would strongly influence your managerial considerations and, most certainly, your chosen solution. But, and here is the nub of the matter, someone lacking your counselling ability and perseverance (and, hence, failing to pinpoint the real cause of the trouble) might well arrive at a very different solution, for example:

> There are no tangible reasons-cum-excuses for Tom's behaviour and, if he doesn't change, he'll just have to go.

or

> It all seems to stem from the baby's birth – but, since no grown man should carry on like that just because he's become a father, he must either pull his socks up p.d.q. or find another job.

Pinpointing the cause is often difficult and troublesome, but it is a vital preliminary step in the time-conscious and effective solution of any problem.

Step 4   Seeking alternative solutions

Nearly all but the most simple of routine problems are capable of a variety of solutions, but it seems to be a fact of human nature that, once *one* solution has been brought to heel, the availability of alternatives is largely ignored. Also, and especially in the prickly field of management, the occasions are rare when one finds a single solution which is totally correct; more often than not, the 'right' solution is the *best* available in all the circumstances – and, by definition, one cannot have a 'best' solution without finding and checking out the alternatives. The root causes of *this* problem of managerial weakness are, without doubt, the hand-in-glove curses of laziness and expediency – and the executive who has any desire at all to spend time wisely will ensure that he seeks and develops a variety of solutions to every single problem, however basic it may appear. To adopt any other than the best solution is to mortgage great dollops of time in the future – when, if you'll pardon my constant reference to the brute, Sod's Law will ensure that a less-than-best solution will come to grief, with dire penalties in terms of wasted time and effort.

Step 5   The nitty-gritty of choosing the best alternative

The business of selecting the best, most practical solution is a process which, in the main, is concerned with sorting out and coming to terms with *constraints* – which, unless one is singularly lucky, will always complicate the issue. For example:

Established custom and practice.
Laws, rules and regulations.
Collective agreements and other contractual matters.
The degree of urgency involved.
The complexity of the solution.
The overall cost involved in financial terms – and, lest we forget, in human terms.
Side effects and repercussions.
etc.

You know, it is only when we go to the trouble of actually listing such constraints that, just perhaps, we get an indication of why so many managers shy away from the task of considering all the alternative solutions – it's hard work! But it has to be done, and when all the constraints have been determined and weighed, the elected best solution will hopefully constitute a wise compromise.

Note that the act of 'compromising' is only one way to solve a problem. For those of us who are blessed with fertile, exploring minds, there is the juicy process of *improvisation* to whet our appetites. Suffice it to say that one not only needs innate wisdom and imagination in order to bring about an innovative solution to a problem, but bags of courage as well. Finally, and yet again, there is the simple, infinitely beguiling and horribly risky *gut-feeling approach*. Enough said.

Step 6   Checking the outcome

On most occasions, a manager's pride (or the basic fear of being caught out) drives him to check on the efficacy of his chosen solution to a problem. However, such checking is usually confined to establishing in very rough terms whether or not things have worked out as hoped and expected. If all is well, the clever guy gives himself a mental slap on the back, and it's the end of the story – but, and here's my point, it jolly well shouldn't be. This is the time to say to oneself, 'Okay, so you were right – but, with hindsight, is it the case that one of the alternative solutions would have procured even better results?' A **frank post-mortem is not a waste of time, it is a foundation exercise** from which wisdom and experience for the future is derived.

I'm sure it's not my pigeon

No reference to the techniques of time-efficient problem-solving can be complete without mention of one more, widely favoured and attractive course of action – passing the buck. Gee, what better way is there of saving one's personal time and energy than ever so quietly sliding a problem on to someone else's shoulders? Consider the crafty manner in which some managers carry out this executive sleight of hand:

> *Manager to his boss*   'Mr Big, I think you ought to know that . . .'
> (*Whereupon the boss, heaving a sigh, takes the problem on board*)

Or, the more direct and calculated approach, usually implemented by the manager who's got the boss in his pocket:

> *With a cunning leer*   'I'm afraid you've got a bit of a problem . . .'

Leaving aside, which one can't, the sheer immorality and bumble-dom of passing the buck, there remains the golden rule which must *always* be applied when deciding who should be responsible for solving a problem: namely, *the closer to the origin of the problem the decision is made, the better*. So, although you never, ever indulge in passing the buck, do stop doing it.

Self-tutorial

Exercise 9

When next you are faced with a clearly defined problem (like this afternoon, or tomorrow?) and, like the good manager you are, take the six steps towards achieving its solution, make yourself a promise. Simply promise that, in addition to checking the outcome of your efforts in the manner I've described, you will do your level best to *quantify* the thing in terms of time; that is, you will ask yourself:

- Whose time, and how much of the precious commodity, was wasted prior to my solution taking effect? Remember, it may not be purely a question of an enforced halt or delay in work pending a solution. People's worry and frustration can bring about an involuntary waste of their time, so think carefully.

- How much time did I waste in actually working out my solution? Remember, there was probably a period of time lost between your recognition that a problem existed and the instant when you started to tackle its solution. Worse still, what about the period of time between the actual occurrence of the problem and your recognition of it – for isn't this your responsibility, and yours alone? It may therefore be that, in asking yourself this question, you will have to take three time periods into account:
  1. Problem occurrence ⟶ Problem recognition
  2. Problem recognition ⟶ Start of work on solution
  3. Start of work on solution ⟶ Solution achieved/ implemented

In urging you to have a serious go at this exercise (and, let's face it, it's the type of task that invites ducking – especially when there's no one around to engage in some knuckle-rapping), my aim is that you should inject your day-to-day thinking with a conscious and lasting appreciation of time.

Think time – and, if you cannot, you might just as well throw this book on the nearest dung-heap.

Memory-prodder 8

You know what's coming. List, preferably on paper, the six steps in the problem-solving process. Go on, *do it!* Check your answer, and congratulate yourself for being so keen.

More apropos of absolutely nothing

Quite literally, one of the gloomiest occasions at work is the shortest day of the year, either the 21st or the 22nd of December, and it is perhaps fortunate that most of us are occupied with thoughts of the approaching festive season around that time. However, in the unlikely event that the next shortest day is marked by your grumbling about the onset of a wintry dusk halfway through the afternoon, take courage, for the worst has already passed! It's an odd fact that the sun sets at its earliest by the clock some ten days *before* the shortest day – so on the 21st/22nd of December you've the satisfaction of knowing that, at the very least, that afternoon gloom is on the wane.

If you are supremely time-conscious *and* thirsty for knowledge, I can only recommend that you seek the reason for this apparent solar eccentricity in the pages of your encyclopaedia, for the explanation is somewhat lengthy and complicated. Interesting, though, isn't it?

9 Catching spanners before they get in the works

Life is an unbroken succession of false situations.
Observer,
Sayings of the Week, 28 April 1957

Woe betide the manager who, on taking up the reins of a new appointment, fails to observe the hallowed tradition of presenting an 'inaugural address' to his staff. Having spent a fair old time chewing the cud on the likelihood of the awaited arrival being more of an arch-bastard than his predecessor, all and sundry will await this first appearance with bated breath – and, when you think about it, who can blame them? For the new manager's part, it's likely that you'll have burned a few gallons of midnight oil working out what you intend to say on such a crucial occasion –and equally likely that you'll include in your spiel something along the following lines:

> ... and I'd like to emphasize, if you have any queries at all, please don't hesitate to seek me out – remember, this is a team effort, and I'm part of it.'

Or, the pearl of them all:

> '. . . my door is always open.'

Ha! In a pig's ear, it is . . . . More often than we care to admit, the 'ever-open door' assurance, however piously expressed, turns out to have just about as much useful effect as spitting into the wind. Time and time again, those who seek the benefit of our wisdom find their way blocked by the combined armour of an indomitable secretary and a firmly closed door to the inner sanctum:

> 'Yes, Joe, I know this is your sixth attempt to see Mr Big – but I'm afraid he's still tied up. Why not try a little later on – say, Friday week, at two?'

If we are totally frank with our executive selves, we like to assure people that we're available at the drop of a hat rather from motives of being seen as 'approachable' than for reasons of administrative efficiency. The inevitable outcome is that subordinates' time is

115

wasted in trying without success to obtain an audience, or, just as bad, our time is wasted on the few occasions when they do achieve entry, by virtue of the fact that we suffer *interruptions* – usually when we can least afford them.

Er, sorry – but can you spare a minute?

The manager who snarls an abrupt negative to such an opener will very soon earn an unenviable reputation as a boorish so-and-so. Thankfully, such rudeness is fairly uncommon, for the simple reason that most of us fall over backwards to be polite, especially to subordinates – and here is the rub. It's just no good opening the interruption sluice-gates by sporting the 'always available' theme, and then, because we're such innately decent people, trying to cope in a nice, civilized fashion with the ensuing flood. The remedy is simple: have no truck with this dubious philosophy and, instead, educate your staff to the effect that, henceforth and emergencies excepted, there will be fixed times in the working day (or week) for the reception of individual queries and the like. Explain the absolute fallacy of the ever-open door, reminding everyone that it seldom, if ever, works – and, believe me, they'll respect you for your frankly realistic approach. I suppose I'd better cap that assurance with one important proviso: namely, that the whole thing hinges on your being available at the published and promised times. One or two fall-downs in that area and, bingo, you'll be back to square one.

Organizing one's subordinates to toe the no-interruption line is only half the battle, for there remains the equally frustrating and time-consuming business of those off-the-cuff visits from your esteemed colleagues – the umpteen occasions when, doubtless drawn by your magnetic personality, Fred, George, Jean and goodness knows who else decide to drop in for a natter. Being sociable creatures at heart and, more to the point, anxious that others, especially colleagues, should see us in that comforting light, we tend to accept (if not encourage) such interruptions as an intrinsic feature of the working day and, where many of us are concerned, actually enjoy the chit-chats that ensue. The long and short of it is that passing the time of day with colleagues (maybe two or three times per day, and at some considerable length) is a luxury which few executives can afford, and which all should seek to minimize. The manager blessed with the outer portcullis of a secretary should school her (or him) into dealing effectively with his socially-minded colleagues:

'Hello, Mr Brown – no, I'm terribly sorry, he's really up to his ears with work at the moment. Do you wish me to interrupt him?'

That little dodge 'Do you wish me to *interrupt* him?' can be really effective in side-stepping all but the most brash of callers. A more direct but less friendly manoeuvre is to have her say:

'I'm afraid he's tied up at present – can I get him to call you?'

When there is no escaping an interruption, the wily and time-conscious manager will have a simple arrangement with his secretary whereby, once a certain period has elapsed, she will either ring through with a spurious call, or enter his office and remind him that something or other has yet to be done. Either gambit is usually effective in triggering the required withdrawal.

I need hardly add that the art of minimizing interruptions is essentially an exercise in tact and diplomacy.

Mr Bloggs, I have a call for you . . .

I tell you what, let's do the fashionable thing and indulge in a spot of line-tapping. Well, why not? By the way things are going, it'll soon be an established business practice – so, come on, just for the hell of it, we'll get in on the act. What follows is an everyday story of manager folk.

The scene is an office, anywhere. John, manager-ordinary, is writing away busily, when, lo, his telephone rings. He lifts the receiver and settles back in his chair.

JOHN: 'Hello, John Nesbit here.'

BOB: 'Hello, John, it's Bob Aspinall.'

JOHN: 'Why, Bob, how are you – haven't heard from you in ages! How's life at Jolly Roger Foods – still turning out the same old mush?'

BOB: 'Yeah, well, y'know how it is, got to keep the population down somehow. Look, I'll tell you why I'm ringing, John. (Let us hope he does.) I was speaking to Arthur Lloyd the other day, and he mentioned that you'd had some dealings with Zelkmann Transport.'

JOHN: 'Good God, Arthur Lloyd – don't tell me he's still around!

What a character, every time I came across him he was nine parts cut . . . What's he up to these days?'

BOB: 'Oh, he's still with Strongmans, although I imagine his days are numbered. But, for all that he drinks like a fish, he's a useful contact – I've had several good deals on tinplate through him. Anyway . . .'

JOHN: 'Yes, sorry, Bob – you were saying?'

BOB: 'It's about this firm of hauliers – Zelkmann Transport . . .'

JOHN: 'What about them, old chum?'

BOB: 'Well, Arthur said that you'd used them several times for your Turin deliveries, and I was wondering . . .'

JOHN: 'He's quite right, but that's only half the story. In fact, they've got all our European business. The old man's pretty thick with Karl Zelkmann, their MD – and, well, y'know how it is, wheels within wheels. . . Anyway, we signed up a full European contract about two months ago. So, what d'you want to know?'

BOB: 'Very briefly, whether or not they're as good as they say. Y'see, we've stepped-up the EEC side, especially to West Germany – and our present hauliers, Ramways of Bolton, just aren't coping. Knowing your involvement in Europe, I thought . . .'

JOHN: 'Too right! D'you know, I'm going hairless trying to keep up with orders from Italy, alone. Everything's wanted yesterday in this neck of the woods.'

BOB: 'Same here – things are really looking up. So, what d'you think, John – are Zelkmanns worth considering?'

JOHN: 'Oh, I should certainly give 'em a try – they've got a pretty big fleet, and they've never had any trouble getting our stuff through on time. I mean, good grief, what's a few cans of beans to an outfit like that – they could put one of your loads in the dashboard locker!'

BOB: 'Come off it – if it wasn't for the subsidies that keep your lot afloat, we'd have you for breakfast. Look, I reckon it's high time we got together for a noggin or two – d'you ever get up to town these days?'

JOHN: 'Now you're talking. I tell you what, I'm due to visit the ivory tower on Tuesday week – how's about we meet up at Dirty Dick's for a pie and a pint, say around one o'clock?'

BOB: 'Sounds good to me – hold on a tick . . .' (*Pages rustle as Bob consults his diary, while John completes his seventh Yorkshire rose doodle on his blotting pad.*) 'Yes, that's fine, I look forward to that. Hey, by the way, how's Jean these days?'

JOHN: 'Very well, thanks, Bob. She'll be glad to know you rang – I can't imagine why, but she's always had a soft spot for you, you old creep.'

BOB: 'Yeah, it's my fatal charm, y'know. Okay, John, see you on Tuesday week at Dirty Dick's – and thanks for the tip on Zelkmanns, I'll let you know how we make out.'

JOHN: 'Fine – nice to hear from you. Bye for now.'

BOB: 'Goodbye . . . Oh, John, are you still there?'

JOHN: 'Yes – what is it?'

BOB: 'I suppose you haven't got Zelkmann's telephone number handy, have you?'

JOHN: 'Lord save us, what next – hold on . . .' (*It is now John's turn to rustle the pages of his diary.*) Yes, here we are – 01 233 4086, that's their head office. Got it?'

BOB: 'Thanks a lot – see you.'

JOHN: 'Cheers, Bob.'

(*John cradles the receiver and, sitting motionless, wonders why on earth he made a lunch date with someone he can't stand, anyway.*)

Now, having eavesdropped on John's conversation, let's get one thing straight. I am *not* advocating that, as a sop to the Great God Time, one's use of the telephone should be restricted to the exchange of coldly staccato, 'business-only' pronouncements – for, with most of us, that would not only be humanly impossible, but it would also spell the end of good working relationships. But, as in all things, there is a limit beyond which, if we are to be *time-conscious*, we should not tread. A modicum of casual chit-chat on the telephone is essential – a virtual torrent of gibble-gabble is nothing but counter-productive and, hence, is *verboten*.

So far as incoming calls are concerned, it's as plain as a pikestaff that a manager should utilize his secretary's skills as a filter for non-essential and unwanted interruptions. If it is thus obvious, why the blazes do so many secretary-blessed executives still find themselves clobbered with unnecessary calls? Be honest, have you ever given explicit instructions to your secretary on her responsibilities with regard to the telephone? And, if you have, before you give that condescending smile, think about how many time-wasters you answered yesterday? To round off this particular salvo of questions, does your secretary really resort to those familiar but extremely effective gambits?

'Would you hold on for a minute – I'll see if I can interrupt him.'

Followed seconds later by:

'I'm very sorry, but Mr Big is tied up at present – may I take a message?'

Or the very handy:

'I'm very sorry, but Mr Big is not available at the moment – may he call you back?'

'I'm so sorry, he's not available at the moment – may I take a message?'

At this point, I think it is necessary to address a word or two to that positive legion of managers (which, I hope, reader, does not include you in its ranks) who cannot, for a wide variety of personally-held reasons, trust their respective secretaries with any of the responsibilities I've mentioned. It is an unfortunate fact that many so-called secretaries are nothing but glorified typists who've been given the title either to satisfy the wretched vanity of the 'managers' concerned, or to attract them to the misnamed job in the first place. One cannot expect, and it would be grossly unfair to require, such employees to assume roles and duties for which they are clearly unsuited. Similarly, as I've more than hinted elsewhere in these chapters, even when a manager sets out to recruit a 'fully-fledged' secretary, he ends up getting exactly what he, as a selector, deserves – and you don't need me to remind you of the oft-disastrous results. So, to all those who haven't got or can't afford that heaven-sent boon of a trusty right-hand (or who have simply puffed-up their typist's job specification out of all proportion, or indulged in dodgy selection), I say this: you're on your own! Since you have no allies in the battle to do more in less time, everything, but everything, is down to you. For starters, obey the golden rules – which, of course, apply to us all.

Golden rules – when making or receiving telephone calls

- Always announce yourself by name, *never* with a mere 'Hello'.
- Restrict yourself to single and composite 'courtesy-business' openers:

    'Hello, Bill, I'm glad you're in – I'd like to pick your brains.'

'Why, Tom, nice to hear from you – how can I help?'

Beware of using such niceties as 'How are you?', for they only invite your opposite number to wax forth in casual chit-chat.

When presented with the advantageous 'Have you a minute?', be sure to squeeze some profit by replying pleasantly 'A little less, in fact – what can I do for you?'

- Always have your diary and scrap-pad *instantly* to hand – not just out of reach, buried under a pile of papers.

- When trapped by a garrulous nitwit at the other end of the line, say something, anything – and hang up in mid-sentence. Oh, yes, tut, tut, but it works.

- Never delay terminating a telephone call by going on and on with those inconsequential 'sweet nothings' – instead, once your business has been concluded, launch straight into a cordial but eminently brisk farewell:

  'Good, thanks for your help, John – 'bye for now.'

  'Mike, many thanks – see you at lunch.'

- And, for those with bruises from telephone bills on the domestic front, imagine *you* are footing the bill for your office calls – it'll work wonders!

They call them 'working hours'

If one persuades a manager to dig out his personal 'Statement of Terms and Conditions of Employment'* and gets him to look at the bit on 'working hours', it's likely that he'll fall off his chair laughing. What? *Working hours?* Once recovered from his spasm, he'll point a shaking finger at an itsy-bitsy rider to the clause, and, so that you are under no illusions, read it aloud in a voice shaking with emotion: 'As an executive of the company, you will be required to work such reasonable periods of overtime as may from time to time be required in the efficient discharge of your duties. This overtime will be unpaid.' Rubbing the salt in, he will then remind you that, unlike the

*In the UK, the 'Statement of Terms and Conditions of Employment' is the document required by law to be supplied to an employee within the first thirteen weeks of service. It is also the document which, in umpteen thousands of cases (particularly where small outfits are concerned), is never so supplied. I wonder why . . .

thirty-seven-hour week enjoyed by his subordinates, he is expected and required to accept an infinitely elastic working stint – that the '9.00 a.m. to 5.30 p.m.' bit on his statement is little more than a sick joke.

All of which we know, don't we – and more, besides. Over the years, this tradition that the manager's day expands to encompass the work to be done has run hand-in-hand with a second 'custom of the job' – namely, the fond expectation and requirement that he should take a goodly part of the office work home with him. Now, I'm not about to propose that these twin practices are offensive in the eyes of the Great Chairman in the Sky, but I am prepared to argue like stink that, to be fair to himself and his loved ones, a manager should do everything in his power to reduce the overload – and the best way to achieve that is to do more work in less time. Which is what this book is all about.

In the next, meat-in-the-sandwich chapter, we are going to wrestle with the crucial business of apportioning and coping quantitatively with time. Up to now, I've restricted myself to throwing your way what I choose to term 'principles' of timely efficiency – and, as I have intimated, we've yet to tackle the grisly business of applying them in practice. BUT before we start on that caper, I'd like to return to these questions of slaving long hours and taking work home – or, conversely and more aptly, to the vital subject of *relaxation*.

It's your duty to take it easy . . .

. . . from time to time. If you are at all inclined to accept the word of another, do so now. For a manager to work at peak efficiency, it is absolutely necessary that he should take a break of at least ten minutes every two hours, and by 'break' I mean a formal switch-off – not a look-see check-up in the general office, or, for that matter, talking intense shop with a colleague. By way of good example, he should not take coffee at his desk, but at a place well removed from the wretched piece of furniture – and, if there is no centrally located coffee bar, let him ensure that his department is the first to create one. Executive ingenuity will always conjure up a handy nook for such a purpose, and good executive wisdom will make certain that everyone in the department makes use of it. There remain two further requirements: drinkable coffee and a strict control of the time thus spent at leisure.

Even if he achieves a logical and profitable approach to the question of break-times, it is nevertheless obvious that the manager faced with tasks requiring urgent attention and rapid decisions will extend his working hours to accommodate them – and/or, of course, take them home with him at the end of the day. At this juncture, I do not intend to mince words: the manager who does this, for whatever 'inescapable' or compelling reason, is the executive who cannot see the wood for the trees. Despite his (your?) protestations that any alternative is pure pie in the sky and impossible to implement, he is completely wrong.

A MANAGER SHOULD PLAN AND SCHEDULE HIS WORK SO AS TO DO ALL THAT HIS JOB DEMANDS DURING THE COURSE OF A NORMAL WORKING DAY

Crikey, I've said it at last – and you had better believe it. Now read on.

Self-tutorial

Exercise 10

One way or another, I've had a fair old bit to say about the secretary who sits in your outer office, hopefully taking everything in her stride, particularly you – your work, needs, foibles and even your occasional downright cussedness. I reckon the time is now ripe to come down to earth and progress a stage further where she is concerned. The purpose of this exercise is to provide you with a practical yardstick, against which you can measure your secretary's actual or potential skills – and, being the keen manager you undoubtedly are, thereby ensure that you reap maximum benefit from her endeavours. So, eyes down, please, for a running audit on your secretary.

Firstly, her practical skills Exactly how good is your secretary's typing and shorthand – and, in the event that her skills are worthy of improvement, what are you doing about it? Using the following brief guide as a basis for your check, consider seriously whether further (and very cheap) training at your local college would be of benefit to her – *and* to you.

Typing

25 wpm

Well, in the unlikely event that her typing speed is around this level, face the truth – you're employing a 'secretary' with office junior's skills. What on earth have you been up to?

35 wpm

This speed represents a very average typing ability, and it is almost certain that you'll be spending some of your valuable time correcting her 'finished' work. Having said that, many secretaries fall within this bracket – and more than a few have definite potential for improvement. Why not have a serious talk with her about further training?

50 wpm plus

Absolutely no worries here, unless, of course, you are not taking full advantage of your secretary's very superior typing ability.

Shorthand

Under 80 wpm

Again, what have you been up to? If ability at shorthand is an essential requirement, all I can say is you've got yourself a bad old selection bargain. By any standards, this is a poor qualification.

80 wpm

Not much better – it's a junior level of qualification, crying out for a further spell of training.

100 wpm

The majority of secretaries fall within this middle bracket of proficiency, and a fair number could do better if given the training chance. Does the job and your ability as a dictator warrant such action?

120–130 wpm

Lucky you – but, be truthful, is she smarting under the burden of insufficient work or your shocking dictation? Remember, the training thing works both ways, and the local college can doubtless offer *you* some help!

130 wpm plus

For gosh, if this specialist level of ability is any indication of your executive standing, I take my hat off to you. Seriously, I jolly well hope the job deserves such proficiency.

124

It goes without saying that it's not the height of diplomacy to barge straight in with the question 'So what are your typing and shorthand speeds, eh? – this is a subject for friendly and tactful discussion over a cuppa.

Secondly, her general knowledge and proficiency   Bearing in mind that your secretary should be nothing less than your highly skilled and knowledgeable right arm, what are her standards in the following general areas – and what are you doing to improve them?

Communication

a   Exactly how good are her powers of written communication? (And, not to put too fine a point on it, while we're on the subject – what are you like at this delicate art?)

b   And what about her abilities as a verbal communicator – remembering that far too many secretaries speak with one voice when addressing people in person, and quite another when using the telephone. How does she perform the vitally important role of acting as your (and the firm's) ambassador?

Human relations

No, a dollop of formal tuition in human relations is not something which is strictly for the birds and squint-eyed trick-cyclists. Consider the questions of relations with the public, fellow employees, superiors, and so on – bearing in mind that, as with every other item in this list, you can get valuable help from local Further Education sources, without breaking the bank.

Legislation

Think in terms of all the legislation affecting offices, factories, employees, and the like – would it not be a good thing for your secretary to acquire at least a working knowledge of this heavy but necessary stuff? Lest you doubt this, note that the office alone is a prime location for accidents, and think in terms of health and safety . . . And what about developing her talents to the point where she could work for you in matters of researching this and that?

In addition to the above, consider your own specialist functions and ask yourself the questions:

'Is my secretary jogging along on the knowledge she has gained merely through working for me? And is this sufficient – or would we both benefit if she underwent some basic training relevant to my lines of activity?

One extremely easy way to toss this exercise out of the window is to give vent to the hoary old *status quo* adage: 'Ah, but things are quite okay as they are – better not to make waves.' If you are a determined sloth-cum-coward, nothing I can say will alter that fact – but, boy, do you have good cause to blush. . .

Memory-prodder 9

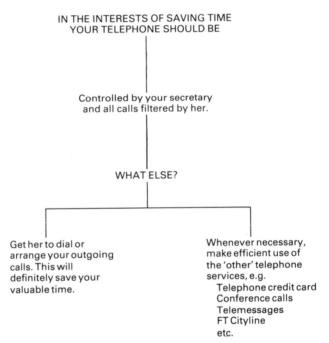

Figure 7   *Using the telephone*

More apropos of absolutely nothing

If there is one thing most of us don't even think about, it is the manner in which the pace of life in general has accelerated over the past thirty or so years. Caught up in the maelstrom we call 'progress', we virtually ignore the frenetic speed at which we are driving ourselves – and make no mistake, our minds and bodies were not designed for such constant over-stimulation. Running on the 100-octane fuel of modern life may be obligatory, but it is a positive cause of fatigue, strain and emotional illness – which is why the enlightened few make absolutely certain that, at regular intervals, they STOP. When last did you do exactly that?

10 Getting the act together

> There are only two qualities in the world: efficiency and inefficiency; and only two sorts of people: the efficient and the inefficient.
>
> G. Bernard Shaw,
> *John Bull's Other Island*

In a manner of speaking, this chapter is the one that puts the lid on all the preceding stuff – and, for this reason alone, it would be gratifying to yours truly if, in some magic way, this introductory spiel could be accompanied by a rousing fanfare of trumpets. It would be even more gratifying if, as I write, I found myself tingling with the knowledge that I was about to reveal a hitherto unknown and completely magic formula for grappling with the Great God Time. Well, I've got news for you: the only tingle I can feel is the onset of writer's cramp – and, surprise, surprise, there is no magic formula. Having led you by the ear through a jungle of hints on how best to utilize the hours in your day, there is no escaping the fact that it's now 'syrup of figs' time. So, brace yourself, and swallow the familiar medicine. Try to believe my assurance that I'll spoon it down your throat as swiftly and pleasantly as possible . . .

To begin with, commit to memory that oh-so-wise line by C.S. Lewis in *The Screwtape Letters*:

> 'The Future is something which everyone reaches at the rate of sixty minutes an hour, whatever he does, whoever he is.'

We are all inclined to make such observations as, 'Goodness, it's the first of the month already – whatever happened to the last four weeks?', and, even as we thus comment on the apparent rush of time (or positive crawl, as the case may be), know that in one sense we are talking arrant nonsense. As Lewis so aptly reminds us, the march of time is unalterable and inexorable in its measured passage. I make no apology whatsoever for quoting the obvious: it is what we do within those precious minutes and hours that determines not only whether they rush or crawl by, but, also, whether we use them as our Maker intended – for each and every second that passes is a fallen leaf off the Tree of Life, totally lost and beyond recall.

Let's get back on track, and have a mighty stab at tackling the effective, quantitative utilization of our working time.

This chapter's hero is Doug

Douglas Rearden, our mythical example-executive, is production manager at Feather-Bed Packings Limited, a medium-sized and successful firm engaged in the manufacture of soft fruit packaging materials and sundry other compressed paper products. Doug, aged forty-three, has spent all his working life in the production side of industry, and enjoys a reputation at Feather-Bed Packings as a good, all-round manager, popular with his workforce and, just as important, respected by his seniors.

Being a man who has never tended to rest on his laurels, Doug spends a goodly proportion of his leisure time musing on ways and means of improving his personal efficiency and, just recently, was spurred by a trivial but, to him, significant event to think even more seriously in this vein. It had all started when one morning in the office, Doug was visited by an ex-colleague and friend, Mark Ayres, an eminently successful career-executive whom Doug much admired for his sheer professional competence and acumen. During the course of a brief but pleasant natter, our hero had had occasion to refer to his desk diary – and, at the time, had taken little notice of Ayres's quip to the effect that his diary entries 'looked like a dog's dinner'. It was only later that Doug, thinking back on the conversation, recalled Ayres's comment and took a critical look at his diary – was it, he wondered, really as bad as all that? If there was one thing that concerned him, it was the question of putting his working hours to the best possible use – and, on glancing again through the diary, he readily admitted to himself that, while he didn't think his entries were *quite* as disorganized as Mark's joking comment had implied, there was considerable room for improvement. (At this point, by dint of hocus-pocus, we can look over Doug's shoulder at a page of his diary – see Figure 8.)

Casting about in his mind, Doug decided that if the diary was to be of any real value in helping him to save time, it should take the form of a detailed daily schedule of his planned activities and, hence, constitute something more than a mere memory-jogger for the odd appointment or item for attention. It would also require

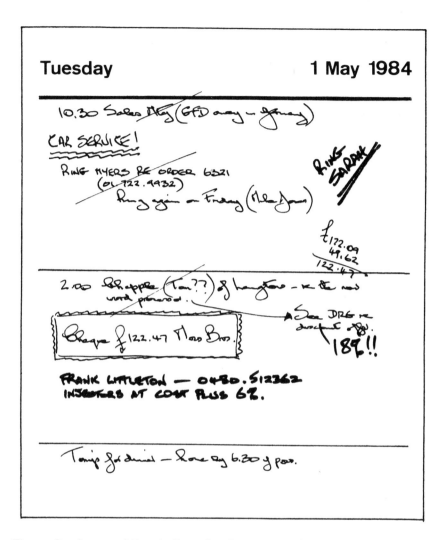

Figure 8 *A page of Doug's diary (by the way, just how much tidier is your magnum opus?)*

to be a mite tidier. That evening, while the family were all out at the cinema, Doug sat down at the dining-room table and, purloining some paper from his student-daughter's notebook, prepared what he regarded as a fairly comprehensive timetable of his planned activities for the following day. Then, pouring himself a well-earned drink, he relaxed in front of the fire – thinking that, if the schedule proved useful, he'd have to buy a larger diary and rule up the pages to make a proper, workmanlike

```
MY WORK-PLAN - THUR 17 MAY 84
```

From	To	Activity
09.00	09.30	Clear outstanding work in In-tray & odd points with Anna - check absentees with Wilf
09.30	10.00	Check with Prog Clk on pos'n of Waverley and Burston apple packings - tour floor & check with Bill on new poly-laminate mach - confirm installation complete to GFH
10.00	10.30	Clear In-tray & sign-up A's typing - phone Merryweathers on pos'n of o/s cartons
10.30	12.30 (?)	MD's meeting - present proposals for poly-laminate prod'n runs (details with A)
12.30 (?)	13.00	Shop stewards' meeting - twilight-shift proposals
13.00	14.00	Lunch - if lucky!!
14.00	14.30	Appt - Jim Dawson on River Mill board order and poss'y of their supplying raw pulp

/14.30   15.30...

Figure 9a   *A typed copy of Doug's work schedule – the first page*

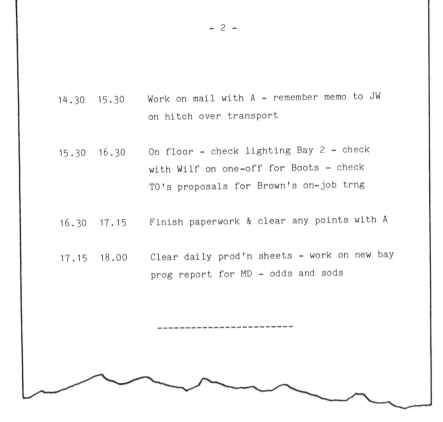

```
                              - 2 -




    14.30  15.30   Work on mail with A - remember memo to JW
                   on hitch over transport


    15.30  16.30   On floor - check lighting Bay 2 - check
                   with Wilf on one-off for Boots - check
                   TO's proposals for Brown's on-job trng


    16.30  17.15   Finish paperwork & clear any points with A

    17.15  18.00   Clear daily prod'n sheets - work on new bay
                   prog report for MD - odds and sods



                   ------------------------
```

Figure 9*b*   *Doug's work schedule – the second page*

journal. (Again, being magically privileged, we can inspect a typed copy of Doug's schedule – see Figures 9a and 9b.)

The next day, Doug arrived early at work and, armed with the schedule, commenced the day with a determined will to make efficient use of the hours at his disposal. Initially, he was much encouraged to find that things went fairly well in that he managed to action all the items scheduled for completion by 10.00, some fifteen minutes before his deadline. However, by 10.30, when he was due to appear at the managing director's meeting, he was a little concerned that he hadn't cleared his in-tray as planned – mainly because the telephone call to Merryweathers regarding the outstanding order for cartons had necessitated a long and tedious conversation and much digging in files. He was not overly surprised when his carefully laid plans were further disrupted by the fact that the MD's meeting dragged on until nearly 13.00, with consequent delay to his session with the shop stewards – but, for all that it wasn't his fault, he felt annoyed that he was failing to keep to the carefully prepared schedule.

The necessity to keep the appointment with Dawson at 14.00 dictated that Doug's lunch was an extremely hurried and scratch affair, but he felt somewhat compensated when, their business concluded in double-quick time, the rep left his office at around 14.15. Doug immediately dived in to the next planned activity, work on the mail – linking this with an attempt to clear the left-overs in his in-tray. By 15.30, the time scheduled for his afternoon tour of the production floor, he'd by no means finished and was particularly concerned over his failure to even make a start on the intended memo to Joe Williams regarding transport difficulties. However, determined to stick to his planned timetable, Doug abandoned the outstanding paperwork and, at 15.32, was deeply immersed in checking the maintenance fitter's alterations to the lighting in Bay 2. Satisfied that all was well, he then proceeded to check with Wilf Archer, his line supervisor, on the progress of the one-off production run for Boots, which had been causing some trouble. This done, he sought out the training officer and, at just on 16.50, concluded his routine check of apprentice on-the-job instruction. Time-wise, things were getting slightly hairy . . .

Once back at his desk, Doug resumed his battle with the paperwork – only just remembering in the nick of time to read and sign the letters typed by his secretary before she left the office for the day. Working steadily without even pausing to light his pipe, he was quite amazed when, glancing at his watch, he found that it was 18.20, well after his accustomed pack-up time. He'd accomplished a great deal during the concentrated and, happily, uninterrupted burst of activity, but his sense of achievement received a severe jolt when he realized, with something of a sinking feeling, that he had yet to complete any work on the report for the MD. Acutely and suddenly aware that his boss would be expecting to receive the document by the following afternoon at the latest, Doug shovelled the relevant working papers into his briefcase and, heaving a deep sigh, departed for home – knowing that he faced a certain two-hour slog later that evening.

Our striving production manager was not in the best of moods when, following the usual hectic drive through the remnants of the rush-hour traffic, he finally arrived home. Much of his discontent centred round the hard fact that he hadn't managed to keep in line with his schedule, and, not a man to accept defeat easily, he determined to seek Mark Ayres's advice on where he had slipped up. So, after dinner and prior to starting work on the report, he telephoned Ayres – and, glad to find his friend only too willing to help, launched into a terse explanation of what he'd tried, and failed, to bring off.

At this point, reader, I'm sure you'll have no difficulty in guessing the bare bones of our mythical Ayres's advice to poor old Doug – particularly if you were sufficiently energetic to have had a go at Exercise 1, way back at the beginning of this book. Yes, that's right; after a timely (no pun intended) reminder that work schedules seldom work out as planned, Ayres plunged straight to the real nub of the matter – *priorities*. He suggested in no uncertain terms that Doug, before going to the length of drawing up any schedule of work to be done, should allocate priority levels to each and every task involved. Not sparing his pal's blushes, Ayres went on to point out that the matter of the overlooked report for the MD was proof positive that, whether he liked it or not, the success of Doug's efforts hinged on this vital preliminary step.

Having thanked Ayres for his advice, our hero hung up and straight away tackled the tedious business of drafting the report for his boss. To his surprised relief, things went very smoothly and, by shortly after 9.30, he had completed what he felt certain was a comprehensive and succinct account of progress to date on the new production bay. Vastly encouraged by the knowledge of a job well done, and still feeling comparatively fresh, Doug remained at the dining-room table – and, digging into his briefcase for the ill-fated schedule, subjected it to close scrutiny. Crikey, he mused, Mark was certainly right – in terms of 'priorities' the list of timed activities was little more than a hotch-potch miscellany of tasks.

Ignoring his wife's plea to join her for the *News at Ten*, Doug remained deep in thought – and, quite suddenly, the penny dropped. He realized that, in compiling the schedule, he had done little more than merely write down what had already been in his mind regarding the forthcoming day – that, even without the formality of the list, he would have engaged in exactly the same activities, in exactly the same order. True, the schedule had served to make him more conscious of the passage of time. At least, he fancied that was the case, but what a wasted effort it had been. Grabbing his pen, Doug decided to have a crack at allocating priorities to the tasks, thinking that,

```
┌─────────────────────────────────────────────────────────────────┐
│                                                                   │
│          MY LIST OF PRIORITIES FOR 17 MAY 84                      │
│                                                                   │
│                                                                   │
│     Using, say, the following scale:                              │
│                                                                   │
│          Priority 1  -  Very urgent/unavoidable                   │
│          Priority 2  -  Urgent/try not to avoid                   │
│          Priority 3  -  Routine/avoidable                         │
│                                                                   │
│                                                                   │
│     Priority 1                                                    │
│                                                                   │
│     (a)  Check with Bill re installation of new poly-laminate     │
│          machinery - GFH waiting for confirmation.                │
│                                                                   │
│     (b)  Phone Merryweathers on delivery position of out-         │
│          standing cartons - required for production.              │
│                                                                   │
│     (c)  MD's meeting.                                            │
│                                                                   │
│     (d)  Write memo to Joe Williams on transport difficulties.    │
│                                                                   │
│     (e)  Check with Wilf Archer on progress of urgent one-off     │
│          order for Boots.                                         │
│                                                                   │
│     (f)  Draft report to MD on progress with new bay - required   │
│          for next day.                                            │
│                                                                   │
│     Priority 2                                                    │
│                                                                   │
│     (a)  In-tray work and signing mail.                           │
│                                                                   │
│     (b)  Check position on absentees.                             │
│                                                                   │
│     (c)  Tour floor at least once during day.                     │
│                                                                   │
│     (d)  Meeting with shop stewards - keep 'em happy.             │
│                                                                   │
│     (e)  Appointment with Jim Dawson of River Mill - shouldn't    │
│          really cancel at short notice if at all possible.        │
│                                                                   │
│     (f)  Check lighting in Bay 2 - it must be finished soon.      │
│                                                                   │
│     (g)  Check with TO re apprentice on-job training.             │
│                                                                   │
│                                                  /Priority 3...   │
│                                                                   │
└─────────────────────────────────────────────────────────────────┘
```

Figure 10a   *A typed copy of Doug's list of priorities – the first page*

136

Priority 3

(a) Check with Progress Clerk on position of Waverley and
     Burston apple packings - production should be well
     under way.

(b) Clear daily production sheets.

(c) Speak to Anna re any odd points.

Figure 10*b*   *Doug's list of priorities – the tail end*

although it was too late to be anything other than a purely academic
exercise, the effort was well worthwhile. Some twenty minutes later,
he was moderately satisfied that he'd done the trick, and, heaving a
rueful sigh, joined his wife in front of the television.

Doug's list of priorities is cunningly reproduced in Figures 10*a* and
10*b*. Have a shot at comparing this with the schedule – and see
whether, on the limited evidence available, you agree with his
findings.

Plainly, in a fairy-tale illustration such as this account of Doug
Rearden's attempts at coping effectively with time, it will be difficult
for you to make anything but cursory inroads into the 'facts' of the
situation. Nevertheless, it is possible to draw some fairly weighty
conclusions – and this is precisely what we are now going to do.

To begin with, I hope you've spotted Doug's sixty-thousand-dollar
omission from his list of priorities: namely, the total lack of any
mention of that very necessary adjunct to good management,

delegation. Next, he has chosen to make ominous use of the terms 'unavoidable', 'try not to avoid' and 'avoidable', and, in so doing, has provided us with something of a clue regarding his general approach to this question of allocating priorities. In sum, Doug has demonstrated his ignorance of two basic rules:

- In setting work priorities, and whenever the nature of the tasks so permit, delegation should *always* be considered.

- The purpose of the game is to decide the order in which tasks are to be carried out, either by the person concerned or by someone delegated to do so, and this is far removed from the crafty business of determining the odds in favour of their avoidance.

A spot of work . . .

I would now like you to plonk yourself firmly in Doug Rearden's shoes, and, using Figure 11 as a basis for your work, have a shot at compiling a new schedule of his work for that fateful day of 17th May 1984. At the end of this chapter you will find some notes on likely pitfalls and snags – but, being the honest Injun you are, I do not expect you to look at these until you have finished. So, no peeping . . .

Having produced your masterpiece and run the gauntlet of the notes, let us now toss poor old Doug back into his fictional limbo, and place *your* hopes and intentions for coping with time on the dissection slab. Do forgive the familiarity, but it's at this point that I much regret I'm not sitting at your side. It would be so much easier for us to work together, instead of my slinging this stuff on to paper in the faint hope that, somewhere, somehow, you, the reader, will manage to get by without benefit of question, query or debate. Still, there it is, you're stuck with this virtual deluge of one-way communication, and all I can do is strive to make my disembodied words as meaningful and descriptive as possible. Crikey, where was I? Ah, yes, we're about to look at you, and *your* approach to the effective management of time – for, after all, it's *you* that counts!

Shake the dice and proceed to 'GO' – do not move beyond 'GO'

There is absolutely no way that you can produce a time-conscious method of working until you have compiled a list of jobs to be done.

```
                      SCHEDULE OF WORK



   From    To      Priority               Activity


   09.00   .....    .....       ................................

   .....   .....    .....       ................................

   .....   .....    .....       ................................

   .....   .....    .....       ................................

   .....   .....    .....       ................................


                          (And so on)


   .....   18.00    .....       ................................
```

Figure 11   *Use the above format for your stab at Doug's work schedule*

By which trite statement I mean quite simply that, from here on, I do not intend to preach a series of lofty principles, for possible application when and if you please. If we're to really work together, then let's do exactly that – and the first step must, perforce, be down to you. Please put this book on one side and, maybe using tomorrow's commitments as a basis for your thoughts, *draw up a comprehensive list of your planned activities throughout a day at work*. We can go no further until this has been done, so do get cracking!

All right? Fine – the next step, as if you didn't know, is to allocate those priorities. for your convenience, I'll repeat Chapter 2's breakdown of typical priority levels:

Priority 1   Very urgent and highly important activities requiring your immediate and undivided attention.

Priority 2   Very urgent but not so important activities which, if you are really pushed for time, can be delegated to others.

Priority 3   Not so urgent but highly important activities which, if pressed for time, can be delegated – thereby ensuring that, at the very least, a start is made on their completion.

Priority 4   Those activities which, lacking urgency or importance, can, if necessary, be shelved, ignored or delegated.

Okay, I would hope that your list of 'personal' activities has been somewhat reduced by the assiduous application of priorities. We now press on to the third stage of planning, where, displaying the utmost courage and fortitude, we come face-to-face with the most deadly of enemies in the battle for time-conscious supremacy – time-wasters. I would like you to consider each item on your amended task-list in the light of its (or, rather, your) susceptibility to the multitude of factors which can impede or prevent its completion. Time-wasters come in a multitude of colours and disguises – and here is a representative list for your digestion:

A confusion of time-wasters

Group 1 – those that are wholly within your power to control

a   Despite your attention to priorities, *failure to delegate*. Are you absolutely certain that the task under consideration cannot be delegated?

b   A *lack of information* essential to the successful completion of a task. Are you confident that your efforts will not be hampered and delayed by insufficient or poor information?

c   *Inadequate responsibility/authority*   Do you, in fact, possess the required levels of responsibility and/or authority to enable you to carry out a certain task? This particular time-waster is included within this group for one very good reason: it *is* within your power to do something about it – either obtain the required improvement or, albeit a serious step, decline to undertake what, in effect, is a hopeless proposition.

d   *Muddled objectives*   Are the aims and objectives of the task crystal-clear in your mind?

e   *Lack of planning* will virtually guarantee a massive waste of time, and almost certainly threaten the final outcome of a task.

140

f *Attempting the impossible*   Whether motivated by an overdose of optimism, undue loyalty, sheer desperation or whatever – it matters little – there are some unfortunates who take on tasks which, in the prevailing circumstances, are simply impossible to bring off with any degree of success.

g *Lack of self-discipline*   This prime managerial disease and time-waster cannot be cured overnight. However many books a manager may read (!!), however many courses he may attend, the hard fact remains that he may fail to change what, in essence, is a serious weakness of personality. But, for all that, we have no choice – it must be included within this first category, for no one but the unfortunate person concerned can bring about an improvement.

Please remember that this is merely a sample list. I urge you to think of further time-wasters which fall squarely under the heading of 'those that are wholly within your power to control' – and it shouldn't take too much thought!

Group 2 – those that, to be fair, are beyond your control
a *Meetings scheduled by seniors*   As you well know, these can be the very devil in terms of wasting time – especially those regular management (more aptly named 'command') meetings chaired by the MD, and the like. When scheduling your activities, of which more anon, try to cushion the 'overlap effect' of a potentially prolonged meeting by inserting non-urgent tasks in the period following that allowed for the session. Ah, yes, and remember to play your time-conscious part at the meeting by being the soul of brevity.

b *Unavoidable interruptions*   When the boss pulls the string, we mere puppets dance ... The unexpected summons to His Nibs's presence can be a very effective time-waster – as, indeed, can be the sudden and important visitor to *your* sanctum. Again, cordial brevity may be the only part-remedy.

c *Failure by others to produce*   When the completion of a task is delayed by the failure of others to come up with vital data, an explosion of wrath may do wonders for your metabolism – but it won't alter the fact that your schedule is up the creek and requires pretty swift amendment. Cut down the time-wasting element by getting to grips with exactly that.

And many others.

A minute ago, I urged you to think of some more time-wasters. However, being something of an old hand at the instruction game, I know that, when no one is looking, such incitements are apt to fall on very stony ground . . . Here is a jumbled batch of further undoubted time-wasters; examine each one carefully in the light of your own experience and consider how best it can be avoided, or, at the very least, it's adverse effect minimized. Hum, and lest we forget, decide in your heart of hearts which of the devils, in whole or in part, are 'down to you':

A restrictive company policy
Cumbersome procedures and practices
Lack of support/interference by seniors
Deficiencies in your administrative (etc.) systems
Poor communication
Lack of adequate staff
Procrastination
Concentration on personal problems
Simple fatigue or other unfitness
Over-keenness on socializing
Inclination to make off-the-cuff decisions
Over-delegation
Poor morale
An over-abundance of mistakes
Hiccups/rifts in working relationships
Fear of seniors, peers or subordinates
Inability to avoid unnecessary interruptions
Tendency to be unduly influenced by others
Lack of support by subordinates
Over-indulgence in idle chit-chat

Hey-ho for scheduling . . .

In my battle-scarred experience, whenever the topic of effective time-management rears its head in group discussion, there is always at least one member who will indignantly splutter something along the lines of:

'Oh, Gawd, Clive, can't you understand that I simply don't have the time to sit down and draw up flaming job-lists, schedules, and all that other junk! It's all very well for you to sit there like a flickerin' Buddha and tell

142

us what we ought to be doing – but you're not at the sharp end, are you? If you were, you'd realize that working life isn't a textbook, with nice, ordered sections – it's just a plain, blinkin' struggle for survival.'

Since you, reader, have persevered thus far with this book, I think it unlikely that you will feel *quite* so emotively aroused; however, I would be a class-one idiot to reject such sentiments out of hand. Of course, it takes time to plan how to save time – but it's the end result that counts. So, if your faith is undergoing something of a beating, take heart – and have your pen ready, for, like it or not, we're going to grapple with schedules, and succeed!

Take a look, if you will, at Figure 12 which illustrates a typical format for a daily work schedule. Examine the layout, knock it around to suit your individual tastes and then have a small supply produced for your initial use. Don't succumb to the temptation of having a thousand copies run off, for not only would that be more than three years' supply, it would be a deterrent against your amending the thing early on – as you may well wish to do.

Before attempting to compile your first real schedule, commit to heart the following tips:

1 Giving due deference to your assessed priority levels, always try to group similar activities together on the schedule, thereby creating a smoother and hence more efficient flow of work.

2 When the need arises to hold meetings or discussions, try like fury to work out specific agendas in advance – and certainly before attempting to schedule such events. This vital preliminary will enable you to allot far more realistic periods of time for their completion, which is needed in order to chair them with any degree of proficiency.

3 Remember that each daily schedule should contain a wedge of time set aside for *thinking* – not, as I've said elsewhere, for the purpose of day-dreaming.

4 Remember, also, to schedule some time for unexpected activities.

5 Never stop thinking in terms of DELEGATION.

6 Note the columns for 'actual times' in the schedule format in Figure 12. Always do your best to record this information, for the success of your efforts will depend on a continuous system of self-audit.

WORK SCHEDULE FOR _____ 198__

Planned times	Priority	Activity	Comment	Actual time
09.00 - 09.15	.....	....	....	......-.....
09.15 - 09.30	.....	....	....	......-.....
09.30 - 09.45	.....	....	....	......-.....
09.45 - 10.00	.....	....	....	......-.....

(And so on, for the entire working day)

Figure 12 *A typical format for a work schedule*

We have now reached the point where, with a terse 'Over to you – from here on in, it's your baby', I retire from the fray and, with fingers and toes crossed, leave you to tackle your first trial period. I can safely forecast that *a* it won't come easily, and *b* you will be strongly tempted to drop the whole tedious box of tricks in favour of those old, attractive ways. Foreknowledge is strength and knowing that you'll be thus tempted should help you to resist Old Nick's blandishments – *for resist you must.*

A word on that self-audit business

Since your policy of getting more done in less time must be one of continuous improvement, it is esential that you carry out regular self-audits of your progress. Plainly, this will involve subjecting your actioned schedules to rigorous inspection – primarily to establish the reasons for discrepancies between the planned periods of time for all your activities and the actual time expended on them. The following self-questionnaire should be uppermost in your thoughts:

1   As events turned out, were my assessed priorities correct?

2   What time-wasters impinged on my efforts – and what can I do to prevent similar occurrences in the future?

3   What tasks did I fail to complete and why? So far as the 'failures' are concerned, what lessons can I learn for the future?

4   What did I do that did not need to be done – by me or anyone else?

5   With the benefit of hindsight, what activities *could* have been handled by someone else?

6   What did I do that wasted other people's time?

7   Did I remember to include within my schedule those vital and revitalizing 'switch-off' periods?

8   What, in sum, has been the measure of my progress – and what am I going to do to ensure continuous improvement?

What indeed? It's all up to you!

Notes on your schedule of Doug's work

Yes, of course, the world is literally your oyster when tasked with the business of compiling a schedule which, perforce, is based on pure fictional ballyhoo – but, for all that, how did you make out? Check your undoubtedly impressive effort in the light of the following general comments and, if they spur you to think further on the question of time-efficient planning – why, good, for that is my intention.

Priorities

Whether you happened to agree with Doug's assessed priorities is pretty academic – what really matters is how did your thoughts run when slotting his various tasks into the day's schedule? As I'm sure you'll agree, there is no one 'correct approach' and, in view of the limited information at your disposal, you could be forgiven for treating the entire exercise in a very arbitrary fashion. However, that aside (and remembering the class-one let-out that you cannot be 'wrong'), did you consider:

a   The underlined urgency of the report for the MD – and the fact that, the earlier in the day Doug completed the beast, the sooner his secretary would be able to start typing it? True, the deadline for the report wasn't until the following day, but would not Doug have derived some advantage if Anna had been able to produce it before finishing work on the 17th – thereby allowing plenty of time for snags or amendments?

b   The good old general principle of scheduling of (as far as possible) top priority tasks early in the day – the 'get them out of the way' approach?

c   The fact that, in your view, Doug's 'scale of priorities' (shown at the top of Figure 10a) were faulty – that is to say, over and above his use of such terms as 'unavoidable'.

Delegation

Well now, having reminded you pretty forcibly about the need to delegate wherever possible, I'm dead certain that your completed schedule excluded several tasks – on the basis that Doug should,

146

indeed, have resorted to the healthy art of delegation. Is my certainty justified?

Apropos of ABSOLUTELY EVERYTHING

It is your unalienable right to question or simply reject anything I have offered in the preceding pages. However, there is one assertion I can make without the slightest fear of correction, and it's this: although I pray it is hull-down on the horizon, that final inevitability, the moment of your death, is somewhere out there – drawing nearer with inexorably measured tread. This above all else is true: your current account balance at the Bank of Time is dwindling with the passage of every minute – and you owe it to yourself to squeeze the utmost benefit from those never-ending debits.

11 Miles and miles of time

> Since railways came into existence, the necessity of not
> missing the train has taught us to take account of
> minutes whereas among the ancient Romans, who had
> not only a more cursory science of astronomy but led
> less hurried lives, the notion not of minutes but even of
> fixed hours barely existed.
>
> Marcel Proust,
> *Cities of the Plain*

It was only recently that a manager-acquaintance of mine chose
to weep copiously in his beer and, between sobs, come out with
a sadly familiar story:

> 'God, Clive, today's been one of those days . . . I had to go up to
> Doncaster this morning to thump the table with one of our sub-
> contractors – so, wanting to get back as soon as I could, I made a
> point of starting out really bright and early. I tell you, Mary nearly
> had a fit – I was away from the house before six-thirty! For once, the
> journey up the A1 wasn't all that bad – the hole-diggers must've
> been taking a holiday – and, oh, I pushed it a bit, because I was in
> the guy's office long before ten o'clock. Then, of course, the trouble
> started. They hadn't done a thing about our order, except get the
> specifications well and truly up the creek – and it took until lunch-
> time to sort that little lot out. It's always the same, give 'em an inch
> and they'll take a mile. Anyway, I got back on the road at just after
> two, by which time it was belting with rain – and what a drive that
> turned out to be . . . All right, I admit I was in a hurry and the road
> was bad, but I haven't seen driving like it since I left the Middle East.
> I nearly got written off at Norman Cross, when some idiot went like
> a bat out of hell straight across my bows . . .'

Encouraged by a sympathetic nod or two from yours truly, Phil's
saga went on and on – to culminate in a graphic description of
how, on his eventual return to the office, he found his in-tray
bulging and, to use his own words, 'everything gone to pot'.
Certainly, if the distracted manner in which he slurped at his pint
was any indication, the people at work must have had a pretty
rattled, travel-weary manager on their hands.

It should come as no surprise that in this chapter we're going
to take a good look at the time-consuming travel scene. So,
reader, if you happen to be a wholly desk-bound wallah whose

149

longest safari is a trip to the loo, well, I guess you're excused this particular parade. But, on the other hand, if you are one of the army of managers who drive, fly or travel by rail in the regular pursuit of their activities, then read on.

There's a long, long trail a'winding . . .

Without doubt, one major post-war development for Willie Executive was the ascendancy of a bright new star in his firmament: to wit, the company car. Quite dramatically and, as your friendly tax-man is well aware, for very good reason, the company-supplied vehicle became – and has remained – the most valuable perk for salary-starved managers. As a natural consequence, this tremendously potent status symbol is seldom left to gather rust in the parking lot; for, when there's a need to travel on business, why, dammit, the thing's there to be used. And, of course, on very many occasions there is simply no alternative – but how many driver-managers use their hours behind the wheel to get in some useful work? No, I'm not advocating that you should attempt to write a thesis (or anything else for that matter) while hurtling along the fast lane, for such a practice would tend to complicate, if not terminate, your executive life. What I am suggesting is that your 30-watt, company-supplied, quadrophonic cassette player can be utilized for other than booming out this week's chart-winner from Slimy Harry and the Spare Ribs . . . .

There is no better time than while driving to listen to the tape-recording you quietly made of your last management meeting, yesterday's tedious session with the sales reps, or whatever. Depend on it, the manager who discreetly records such verbal get-togethers is powerfully placed when it comes to making subsequent tactical decisions – and the privacy of one's car affords an ideal opportunity for digesting exactly what was said, and laying plans accordingly. Incidentally, but just as important, what about laying in some of the better quality teach-yourself cassettes which are freely available on a variety of management themes? Music may have charms to soothe a savage breast, but it doesn't do much to improve one's management expertise.

Before we go any further, I think I should get one thing straight. As one who, over the years, has endured more than his

150

fair share of grimy, stinking, uncomfortable commuter trains, I hold no particular brief for British Rail – except, that is, my belief that its one glory, the HST InterCity system, does represent the best means of surface travel between a good many points on the map. So, here's a thought for the day: instead of leaping gaily into that tin heap of a status symbol and scorching off up the motorway (as and when the weather and those everlasting, botch-up repairs permit), why not think in work-effective terms and, whenever possible, elect to travel by train? Yes, I know it's all beginning to sound like one of those glowing full-page ads that British Rail are currently tossing our way, but the fact is we do tend to regard business travel with something approaching tunnel vision (no pun intended):

'Go by train? What – with that luvverly, shining beast sitting out there? You must be joking.'

'So what, pray, do I do when I get to the other end?'

'Look, it's far easier to just get in, turn the ignition – and away!'

'If I don't use the car, they'll take it back.'

Or, since truth will out, we just don't think about it at all – which, of course, was the case with Phil. It was only after the event and over the second pint that he and I got down to brass tacks:

Salient features of Phil's journey

For argument's sake, he left home at, say	06.30
And arrived at the sub-contractor's at, say	08.45
Then, following his lengthy cut-and-thrust, he departed from Doncaster at, say	14.00
And arrived back at his office at, say	17.00

Ergo, he was behind the wheel for a total of 5 hours and 15 minutes. And the work he achieved during this time was *Nil*.

After a few 'ums' and 'ahs', and the production by the landlord of a well-thumbed timetable, we discovered that poor old Phil had really let himself in for a very dicey, exhausting and ill-chosen mode of travel. Instead of cleaving away from home at 6.30 a.m., he could have nestled in bed for a while longer, enjoyed a far more leisurely shave and breakfast, and left the house at around 8.00 a.m., *en route* to the office for a quick suitable work for the journey, he could have driven to Peterborough station in good time to catch the 09.41 'fast train' to Doncaster, arriving at 10.32, a journey time of 51 minutes. If Phil had wanted to pull rank on his recalcitrant sub-contractor, he could have made a prior arrangement to be met at the station – but, for the purpose of our exercise, we decided that a taxi would have sufficed, plonking him at his destination at about 10.50.

True, our planning in retrospect failed to allow Phil as much time as he had actually spent thumping the table with the sub-contractor, but he readily agreed that, had he had a 'target time for departure' in mind, he could have fitted everything in. So, to cut a longish story short, we had our travelling hero back at Doncaster station, clambering aboard the 15.26 to Peterborough, arriving at 16.18 – another 52 minutes which could have been expended on work in warmth and comfort. A quick trot to his car (he wouldn't have got *that* wet...), and back to the office – where he would have had more time *and* the energy to deal with the bush fires and crises that had occurred.

Okay, so anyone can knock up such an example. But, let's face it, those glossy advertisements do tell more than a modicum of truth. There are very many business trips which can be accomplished far more efficiently and in much greater comfort if the decision is made to dump the car and go by train – and, ever conscious of the value of time, get some work done during the hours thus spent. Lest you are inclined to think of the expense of such travel, just recall that little exercise you dutifully carried out earlier on, and remember the cost to your employer of those wasted hours behind the wheel.

Kindly fasten your seat-belt and observe the 'No Smoking' sign . . .

For the not-so-fortunate souls among us, there is a regular requirement to undertake business trips by air – and, if you're one such executive, you'll know exactly what I mean by not-so-fortunate . . . The once-a-year, all-agog passenger who travels the clouds to the Costa del Concrete may find the flight a thrill – but, to the no-choice regular traveller on business, the gilt will have long since worn off. Those airport sausage-machines, designed with the single aim of stripping John Doe of his human lard and rendering him down to an inanimate, unprotesting lump, are bad enough. Add to this iniquity the plastic smiles, plastic food, mightily swollen

152

feet and enervating jet *ennui* – and, no, there isn't much pleasure in the game. But business travellers have to travel – and, if they're wise, always with a view to extracting maximum work profit from their seven-mile-high challenges to gravity. The question is what kind of work?

If you happen to be one of the privileged few who, by virtue of grandly senior status, can elect to travel 'sleeper seat' or 'two abreast' in, say, the Crown First or Superclub Class of a British Airways 747, you'll be more than used to the additional inches provided for your seated comfort – and you should find little difficulty undertaking any form of written work. But, aha, if you're an absolutely top-notch air traveller, accustomed to nothing less than the Mach 1-plus style of Concorde, why, you'll be painfully aware that, so far as written work is concerned, you might just as well leave your pen at home – unless, that is, you are a contortionist, to boot. As for Club and Tourist Class travel, well, any success will depend on your ability to 'lap-write', or your mastery of that infernal tray contraption which, if it deigns to snap open, never fails to knee-cap its taller victim. We'll return to the art of 'writing on the move' in a moment.

Whether it is because of the physical constraints on the airborne executive, or his closer proximity to the Great Chairman in the Sky when aloft, I don't know – but it seems to be a fact that many managers devote the slowly passing hours to thinking. Now this is a splendid and very necessary activity, but, harking back to what I've said earlier, such thinking sessions have to be highly disciplined, logical processes if they are to be of any value at all. There is nothing like the ultra-dry atmosphere of the pressurized cabin and the stultifying hiss-cum-whine of the jets to induce a category-one daydream – to be followed swiftly and inexorably by zzz . . . Remember, also, that jet-lag on long flights starts to appear after the first few hours – so, if there is work to be done, get it completed in the early stages of the journey.

A DIY work-kit for the travelling businessman

Think about how you equip yourself for efficient 'work in transit'? Do you merely sort out your papers, check you've got a pen and snap the jolly old briefcase shut? If so, and if you're at all interested in improving your comfort and efficiency while working on the move, consider the following:

Travelling by train

These days, most train carriages are of the 'open plan' type, equipped with those tables behind which one is required to wriggle when getting in or out of the seat. Now, at first glance, it might seem that these munificently supplied items of furniture are ideal when it comes to written work – but are they? In addition to bearing their usual load of grime, which doesn't exactly help the erstwhile worker, they just happen to be positioned in such a way that every word one writes attracts surreptitious peeps from one's fellow-travellers. The average British passenger may be notorious for his disinclination to pass the time of day (and thank God for small mercies, says this very average Britisher), but his eyes are everywhere!

In order to combat the above and, in any event, to improve writing comfort, I strongly recommend that your briefcase is equipped with one of those clipboard efforts, which are easily and cheaply available from most stationers. You should find, as I do, that this simple item rests nicely against the edge of the British Rail table, providing a clean and conveniently private writing surface at just the right angle. Needless to say, use the bulldog clip as intended, otherwise your work will end up six feet away, under the feet of that ferocious-looking fat lady . . .

Travelling by air

Unless you wish to guarantee knocking your, or your neighbour's gin and tonic for six, don't equip yourself with a clipboard for airborne writing. Instead, make certain that your DIY work-kit contains a stiff-backed notepad of the type used by your secretary for dictation – it should suffice.

By the way, I'm constantly assured that, in these days of pressurized cabins, there's no danger of nasty little mishaps with fountain pens and ball-points. All I'll say is this: my last landing at London Airport must have over-excited my Parker, because it promptly emptied its bladder all over my white shirt – I suppose that's what comes of flying Air Chance . . .

The rest of the DIY work-kit consists of pretty obvious stuff, and I'm sure your briefcase contains every item – or does it?

- *Miniature stapler* Essential for you-know-what, but useless if it is empty and these small staplers run out very quickly – so carry replacement staples!

154

- *Calculator* There was once a time when a certain type of manager advertised his self-assessed importance by sporting a seventeen-function, electronic chiming Wurlitzer of a wristwatch. Nowadays, this trend (in which, of course, you take no part) has changed, and the imagined badge of high office is the scientific calculator; the greater the number of programmable intricacies, the more lavish the display – and, *ergo*, the owner is convinced that he is successfully advertising his personal eminence in the overall scheme of things. All that aside, a carefully selected calculator is a boon to most managers, and should form part of his travelling kit. However, if, like me, Nature has endowed you with spade-end fingertips, do be wary of those credit card-sized items –which may well be first-rate examples of electronic wizardry, but sheer hell to use with any degree of accuracy.

- *Small edition of your desk diary* The much-travelling manager should faithfully maintain the chore of keeping a small duplicate version of his desk diary in his briefcase, for the simple reason that his secretary must always have access to the latter when he is away. True, there is probably a duplicate – but, bosses being what they are, there's bound to be the odd (usually vital) entry that doesn't get transcribed.

- A *'think-book'* If profit is to be derived from those thinking sessions, ensure that you keep a special notepad in which to record your mental products. For your eyes only, this personal version of Chairman Mao's Thoughts for the Day will help no end in formalizing your thinking, and is a whole heap better than the odd, cryptic entry in a diary. Adopt the six-step problem-solving technique, and so discipline yourself that your entries faithfully reflect this approach.

So you think you've got it taped?

Beseiged and tempted as he is by umpteen manufacturers pushing their respective versions of the pocket dictating machine to end them all, one cannot really blame the travelling executive who feels he's morally bound to dump the entire contents of his briefcase in exchange for one such electronic gizmo. Just imagine, there comes that momentous occasion when, firmly ensconced on the 8.03 commuter-bin to town, and thinking in terms of a spot of dictation,

Willie-Manager looks cautiously round at his fellow passengers – and oh-so-casually produces his new toy. Before he's had a chance to mutter a blushing word into the mike, seven pairs of eyes turn accusingly in his direction, daring him to commit such a flagrant breach of the peace. Thus squashed, the poor guy pretends he was only really checking the thing's switched off, and hastily puts it away. On the second travelling occasion, armed with some Dutch courage and a cassette of verbal notes, Willie decides to placate the accusing orbs by merely *listening* to the tape – surely that won't offend? Inserting the earpiece into his left ear, he presses the play-back button and relaxes in his seat – man, this is the executive life! Within seconds, a runny-nosed urchin in the corner seat roars into action: 'Look, Mum – that old geezer's list'nin to Top o'the Pops!' The pairs of swivelling eyes become laser beams and, in a trice, Willie is scorched into abject submission. Red as a beetroot, he crams his Niko-San Electro-Log Mark 22 back in his briefcase, and spends the rest of the journey miserably contemplating his navel.

All of which is somewhat unfair and, hopefully, larger than life. The fact is, given that you possess the particular trait which enables you to make full use of a pocket recorder (for one reason or another, many of us dislike speaking into a mike, whether in company or alone), the device can be very useful when working on the move. Do remember, though, when it comes to actual dictation, care has to be taken that extraneous travelling noise does not impinge on the recording to the extent of torturing a poor typist's ears. And, for goodness sake, speak the speech plainly, and *not* trippingly on the tongue!

Just for the record, most airlines permit their passengers to use tape-recorders and dictating machines, provided that these are not used for the playing of music – which, of course, you would never dream of doing. If, however, you are the proud owner of an ultra-sophisticated tape recorder-cum-radio-cum-anything else, don't try to use it when travelling by air – unless, that is, you wish to sabotage the aircraft's navigation equipment and, by so doing, land in the pokey (and probably Red China).

An ounce of planning is a must

When it comes to the crunch, every hint, tip and scrap of advice in this book should be overlaid with a single, repetitive message, printed in letters six feet high: IN THE FINAL ANALYSIS, IT'S DOWN TO YOU. Would you believe, some management authors are dyed-in-the-wool evangelists, who, having cast their bread upon the water, will retire to their private sepulchres and offer prayers for the conversion of the unenlightened. If I do pop into retreat, reader, it will not be to pray for your management soul, but simply to count my money. So, as I get all fired-up to tell you about the need to *plan* the efficient use of travelling time, let me remind you once again – in the end, it's down to you.

> My God, he doesn't half go on – talk about making mountains out of molehills. If I decide to do some work during a journey, I'll shove everything I need into my briefcase – and, when the time comes, just get on with it. Why all this guff about planning? Blinkin' authors – they're all tarred with the same brush . . .'

Let's imagine that you are actually facing a business trip – and, right at this moment, you're sitting at your desk, all poised to grab this and that bunch of papers with which to occupy yourself on the journey. It may well be that burning priorities will dictate what ends up in your briefcase; but, where some choice is possible, remember one thing. When travelling cheek-to-jowl with fellow-passengers and constantly subject to the jerks and mini-bounces of motion, most of us find it much easier to *read and digest* rather than engage in handwriting. Poking home the obvious, time spent on the move usually presents an ideal opportunity for grappling with wordy reports and the like, as opposed to scrawling reams of travel-jogged composition. By all means, resort to the pen; but if you're one of Nature's scantily-endowed writers, to whom the art never comes easily even in the best of conditions, plan to tackle your stuff in economic, telegraphic lingo – with the aim of putting flesh on the skeletons when you return.

Incidentally, this is an opportune moment to remind you of one administrative practice which is utilized to extreme lengths in government departments but is seldom used elsewhere; and it's a shame because, in addition to being a handy aid to the desk-borne executive (when used in selective moderation as part-and-parcel of an office system), it can be a boon when working on the move. I refer to the humble minute sheet – the blank page which, inserted in the front of every file in the outfit, is used to record notes of action or instructions regarding specific enclosures. So, instead of scribbling in the margin of a letter floating around loose on his desk (as is so often the case), a boss using the minute sheet could deal with the neatly filed article thus:

M.7 (the consecutive number of the minute concerned)

JHK (the intended recipient)

Please see E.23. (The numbered enclosure) This is a pretty serious complaint, but I'm not satisfied that Brown's estimate of the damage is correct. Kindly let me have your views.

GDG (Manager's initials)   10.8.84

To which jewel, JHK, sitting on the 10.30 InterCity to Leeds with the file in his lap, might well pen the reply:

M.8

GDG

Your M.7/E.23. Estimate caters for main bearing replacement and is about right – but hopefully it's not our baby. If, as I suspect, the bearing failed due to oil starvation, likely cause was either user negligence or oil pump failure. Unfortunately, impact damage drained system and rendered on-site inspection of oil pump impossible. Am awaiting lab reports on residual oil samples and strip-down of pump, which should be available within 10–14 days. Suggest Brown is trying to jump the gun – possibly because he also suspects his people were negligent! Will keep you informed.

JHK   13.8.84

Far be it from me to suggest that you go overboard with this business of minute sheets, but there's little doubt that the system can, and very often does, produce order out of administrative chaos – especially for the peripatetic manager!

Back to our topic – the planning of one's work-on-the-move. Plainly, it's not much use Joe Bloggs licking his lips, say, in anticipation of an uninterrupted session of airborne problem-solving if, once swallowed by a Jumbo and four thousand miles away from his desk, he finds that he's set out *sans* a piece of paper containing the one vital key to the entire shooting-match. You may think this is a blatant example of my teaching you to suck eggs, but just consider: how often, when sitting at your desk and grappling with a problem, do you leap out of your chair in pursuit of this or that file or document – simply because, without the wretched thing, you're at a standstill? It happens and, what's more, you know it does. It's a hard fact of executive life that the second step in the one and only approach to problem-solving – yes, that's right, *gather all the relevant facts* – is the single biggest pitfall for the unwary. It is the wise manager who, recognizing his or her weaknesses, resorts to a mini-checklist before zooming off into the wild, blue yonder:

- Do I have all the *paper-facts* to hand which are central to the issue, or am I dodging the task of gathering such information by handily indulging in *assumptions*?

- Is this a problem I'll be able to tackle while travelling, or is there a distinct chance that things will come to a grinding halt because of the need to consult somebody or other?

- And, bearing in mind the confined space when travelling, is this a problem that requires a desk-top to accommodate the many bits of paper involved – and, if I do deem it as such, am I sure this is not just an excuse for dodging the issue?

Something on the theme of brown paper bags

Having (we hope) been spared the money-squandering, ill-designed and stomach-turning tilt of British Rail's Advanced Passenger Train, it seems likely that UK managers will continue to enjoy going by puffer without any significant incidence of travel sickness. Unfortunately, one cannot say the same where flying is concerned; for, to many of us, those airborne bumps and lurches spell, at the very least, unease – and, all too often, absolute work-stopping misery. Ugh . . .

The trouble is, while there are umpteen, fairly esoteric preparations available with which one can seek to forestall air sickness, they pretty well all produce a kind of mentally stupefying side-effect. A crafty dosage may persuade a rebelling tum-tum from galloping up its owner's throat, but the patient is unlikely to be in any fit state for accurate, time-effective work. Do you really need me to tell you that, despite all our hyoscine, antihistamine, cyclizine and goodness-knows-what-based highly priced nostrums, there is no sure cure for the travelling heebie-jeebies?

There are, of course, some fairly obvious precautions to be taken, like not over-eating before and during the flight. This does not mean going without food entirely, which is asking for trouble – usually in the form of an early attack of what are quaintly but aptly termed the 'dry heaves'. As for quenching one's thirst, alcoholic and fizzy drinks are best avoided, particularly if the sickly passenger wishes to avoid putting on a spectacular display during his frenzied rush to the loo. Fresh air is a great help, but since it is somewhat difficult to step outside for a breather, the next best thing is to maximize the flow from the overhead vents provided for just that purpose. Lastly, avoid looking at anything in motion – which, come to think of it, is pretty superfluous advice when it is one's entire, nauseated inside that is whirling around like a demented dervish.

Oh, yes, a postscript for the specific attention of those never-say-die merchants who, sensing the onset of travel sickness, are too proud to admit, even to themselves, that they are thus prone to the malady. Don't just sit with gritted teeth until the fateful moment comes when you discover the hard way that the brown paper bag is woefully inadequate – especially if you're seated next to me!

Bon voyage – and much strength to your travelling labours!

160

12 It'll all come out in the wash

Ah! the clock is always slow;
It is later than you think.

> Robert Service
> *It is Later than You Think*

As far as I'm aware, there are but two near-traditional approaches to the business of rounding-off the final pages of a text book. One method, much loved by authors who believe they should keep the mortars of knowledge firing fresh salvoes at the reader right up to the last full stop, is to do exactly that. The other approach is to present the final chapter of their work as a kind of *pot-pourri* summary of all that's gone before, usually in the blissfully academic hope that the bright-eyed student will thus benefit from regurgitated facts and data. Both methods leave me absolutely cold, mainly because I think they're founded in an outdated and dry-as-dead-bones philosophy: namely, that *a* textbooks should be for learning and never, ever, for entertainment, and *b* there is no such beast as the seeker-after-knowledge who can become bored with his lot. Let's face it, managers at the overworked sharp end are usually too damned tired at the end of their daily grind to engage in an undiluted tedium of study. There has to be a better way of presenting a final chapter and, having loftily disavowed tradition, I guess it's up to me to find it . . .

I know, thinks Goodworth, let's have a happy ending!

A time and place for everything

In introducing you to the mythical Don Street (all right, Sod's Law will ensure there's a reader by that name), it's not my intention to present you with a kind of Boy's Own, clean-cut management hero who, try as he might, can't do anything wrong. To attempt that would be ridiculous – and, in any event, since I've modelled my character on a real-life acquaintance, he must obviously reflect that anonymous and unwitting donor's fair share of human frailties. But, and here's the crunch, for all his various failings, Mr Manager-Street possesses

163

one sterling virtue – and, by all that's holy, you'd better be on the look out for it. Now let's cut the cackle and get on with it.

Don is personnel king within a parent company controlling eight widely diversified subsidiaries – and, as such, is directly responsible for the design and implementation of personnel and training policies throughout the organization. His was the first such appointment and, prior to his taking up the cudgels (an event which caused some rancour among the autonomy-minded subsidiary managements), each company approached the questions of personnel and training in its own, highly individual manner. One or two were sufficiently enlightened to employ a personnel officer, but the others – all fairly large companies – were perfectly content to leave such esoteric matters in the sweaty hands of line management. As is usually the case, there were good and bad reasons behind Don's appointment. On the one hand, some of the subsidiaries had reaped pretty hefty industrial tribunal complications – which, if nothing else, indicated a crying need for a measure of professional personnel expertise. On the other hand, the group's ebullient chief executive, badly infected with organization vanity, wished to fill his ivory tower of a headquarters with a suitably impressive arsenal of centralized specialist services – and the creation of Don Street's appointment realized part of this uncommendable ambition.

From the outset, Don knew full well that, if he was to succeed, his main objective had to be the two-fold aim of destroying the 'ivory tower' image and convincing the hard-headed and alienated subsidiary managements that his appointment was, in fact, worth the hefty slice of their profits that it cost. Eighteen months have now passed, and the group's personnel and training specialist has worked assiduously towards the fulfilment of that objective.

To complete this mini-picture, Don, now aged thirty-eight, is a member of the Institute of Personnel Management, a qualification which he achieved after a lengthy part-time course at college. Having commenced his career as a personnel clerk, he has attained his present status by dint of sheer hard work (plus, of course, the very necessary favours from Lady Luck), and, in addition to his IPM membership, is an exam-qualified member of the Institute of Administrative Management. Married to Gail and a good father to their two young children, he feels that his life is on the up-and-up – albeit that, at times, he tends to get into something of a lather over what, to him, are the very real perils of the rat-race.

164

There, then, is the potted introduction to our subject for the next few pages. Your task (oh, yes, I'm afraid it's yet another job of work) is to take up that supremely handy vantage point of a fly on the wall of Don's office, or wherever else a fly may go. In point of fact, you're about to become a super-gifted fly – because, in addition to witnessing all that transpires, you will also be privy to the working of Don's mind, and the thoughts of others. So eyes down for the eavesdropping exercise to beat them all . . .

0850   Don arrives at work. In order to reach his own sanctum, he has to traverse the open-plan personnel office, where one or two of his staff have already arrived. Nodding pleasantly, he passes the time of day with them – and, remembering that Bob, the junior clerk, has just returned from holiday, asks him how he enjoyed Majorca. Don then enters his office and straight away seats himself at his desk. It is his invariable custom to use the first few minutes of the working day indulging in what he fondly terms his 'private hair-down session' – and, leaning back in his chair, he carries out a swift mental review of the events of the previous afternoon, seeking in his own way to audit the general outcome of his work. Let there be no misunderstanding, Don is not a text-book miracle of a manager, merely a guy who, being deeply interested in his job (and his progress), seeks continually to monitor and improve his personal effectiveness. However, since he is only human, it is not long before his thoughts stray, and, grasshopping with its inexplicable capability from one topic to another, his mind suddenly turns to the casual events of earlier in the day – the breakfast natter with Gail, the playful rough-and-tumble with the children, and so on. Once or twice during this reverie, and almost without knowing it, he glances at his wristwatch – and it's not by sheer chance that, just as the minute hand reaches the hour, he brings his 'session' to an abrupt close.

09.00   Leaning forward, Don reaches for his desk diary and turns to the current page. It is a fairly large diary and, using your *Calypterae's* compound eyes to splendid advantage, you see that the open page has the day divided into half-hourly segments, with the time period (09.00–09.30, 09.30–10.00, etc.) entered against each segment. And the page is also divided vertically, and bears three section headings: 'Task',

'Priority' and 'Notes' – interesting, you think, the guy is plainly a nit-picking pen-pusher.

You watch Don as, scanning the first few entries, his thought-waves are picked up by your ultra-sensitive antennae.

Let's see, now – I've got Tom Smithers coming in at ten o'clock, and the shop stewards at eleven – hell, that's a couple of top priorities on the trot, almost as dicey as yesterday afternoon ... Thank God, Tom's always pretty businesslike, but the union'll try to stretch things out – they always do. Still, I reckon an hour should be long enough ... Hope the mail's on time for once – but it doesn't really matter, there's the journal proofs to be getting on with ... It's gone nine, I'd better make a start ...

For his sins, Don is editor of the group's house journal, a chore that he much enjoys. Conscious that the corrected proofs have to be at the printers by the end of the week, he takes the bundle of papers from his in-tray and is swiftly immersed in wielding his editorial blue pencil.

09.08   Two things happen virtually simultaneously: Jennie, Don's extremely capable secretary, enters with the morning mail and, as she approaches his desk, the telephone rings. As is her custom when she is with her boss, she has switched the phone through to Don – and now, placing the mail in his in-tray and murmuring a quick greeting in his direction, she answers the call. Without thinking, Don places his desk diary within her reach, and then carries on with his work.

After a brief but courteous exchange of words, Jennie consults the diary and says to the caller 'I know that Mr Street will be glad to see you, Mr Carruthers – shall we say next Tuesday, the 21st, at ten o'clock?' ... 'All right – it's been nice speaking to you, Mr Carruthers. Goodbye, and thank you for calling.'

Replacing the receiver, she addresses her boss: 'That was the rep from Ironstone Printers, Don. If you recall, you said you wanted to see him about the new index cards – so I've booked him in for next Tuesday. Now, how about coffee?'

'Yes, please, Jennie!' Don replies gratefully. 'By the way, what did you think of the show – it was last night, wasn't it?'

She smiles. 'Yes, and we both enjoyed it very much. Tim

asked me to remind you that they're doing *The Pirates of Penzance* next month – would you like me to book some tickets?'

'Hey, that's a good idea – I'll speak to Gail tonight and let you know.'

Don returns her smile and, as she turns to leave, he places the journal proofs on one side and reaches for the mail in his in-tray. The small pile comprises seven, folder-type files, five of which are blue (denoting that they are personnel department files), one is yellow (the colour allotted to head office accounts), and the remaining folder is a distinctive red – announcing to all and sundry that it emanates from the office of the chief executive. Being a pretty with-it fly in terms of office systems, you are faintly surprised to note that all the files are of the old-fashioned variety, with their contents hole-punched in the top, left-hand corner and held in place by means of treasury tags threaded through the front and rear covers of each folder. Then, as Don turns his attention to the red file, you see that the front cover, in addition to bearing its boldy marked reference number, has a series of printed columns, headed as in Figure 13.

You realize that this simple system enables the person dealing with a file to refer a specific minute (remember?) or enclosure to the intended recipient – who, when he has completed the required action, will cross out his initials and then, if required, annotate the front of the folder with the initials of the next person in the chain. As Don opens the file, you also realize that, old-fashioned or not, the threaded treasury tag enables the enclosures, all numbered in

REFERRED TO	DATE	MIN/ENCL	REFERRED TO	DATE	MIN/ENCL
JDH	6/5	M1			
PP	May	EA			
JDH	8/5	M.2			
CP	2/7	E20			
GP PERS MGR	13/8	M3/E21			

Figure 13 *File cover*

167

sequence, to be retained on the 'right-hand side' of the folder, while the other end of the threaded tag retains the vital minute sheets (hole-punched in the top, right-hand corner) in a handily accessible position just inside the front cover.

Noting that Minute 3, concerning Enclosure 21, has been referred by the chief executive for his attention, Don reads the short missive:

M3

Gp Pers Mgr

Re. E21. I think we should support the Chamber in this, but since I'm away on 7 September, I'd like you to attend on my behalf – what about a short talk on the new medical scheme?

Let me know your decision.

FAB   13.8.84

You give a quiet, fly-type chuckle as, watching Don peruse the enclosure, you tune in to his thoughts.

Just my luck – trust the old man to duck out of a speaking engagement, especially at the Chamber of Commerce... Well, if I've got to do it, the medical scheme's as good a topic as any... Yes, something on the lines of the difficulties we had in publicizing the thing – the reaction to change and so on... Better check the date first, though – yes, and get Jennie to dig out all the bumph.

Swinging into action, Don opens his desk diary and, having checked the date, makes an appropriate note of the task. Then, returning to the minute sheet, he pens a swift acknowledgement to his boss (constituting Minute 4), crosses out his initials on the front cover, and makes a fresh entry – referring the file back to the chief executive.

But wait – what is Don up to now? You watch as, taking a red pen, he makes a *second* entry on the file cover – this time, referring the file back to himself on 3 September, with Minute 4 marked for his attention. Aha, a smart cookie, you murmur, realizing that Don is taking advantage of the office 'bring forward' system as a belt-and-braces reminder of his enforced public speaking engagement. You need no reminding that, alerted by Don's entry in red ink, the member of staff responsible for maintaining the chief executive's filing system will enter the need to produce the file in his 'bring forward' diary – and, bingo, it will duly plonk into the personnel manager's in-tray on 3 September, just as he requires it.

Don speaks into the office intercom. 'Jennie, when you've got a moment I'd like you to let me have the file on the setting-up of the medical scheme – and, yes, a copy of the booklet we sent out, please. It's not urgent – any time today will do. Thanks.'

You settle yourself more comfortably on your six legs as Don transfers his attention to the remaining folders. Four of these contain letters which arrived in the post earlier this morning, and it pleases you to see that his secretary obviously wouldn't dream of letting her boss get his fingers on any item of business correspondence before it had been allocated to the appropriate file – the new enclosure being duly numbered and, where necessary, cross-referred to earlier papers on the same topic.

Don appears to be lucky – for, with the exception of Jennie bringing in his cup of coffee, he manages to deal with almost all of the in-tray paperwork without any interruption. Two of the letters require a dictated reply, and he places these files one one side – thinking as he does so that, with luck, he'll be able to get in a spot of dictation before Tom Smithers arrives at ten o'clock. He is penning a minute on the last personnel file in the batch when Jennie comes through on the intercom.

She speaks quietly: 'George Boon has just come into the office . . . At present, he's talking with Bob – but, just in case, are you tied up?'

Knowing Boon, the company secretary, as an inveterate gossip, Don is swift to reply: 'Oh, crikey, yes – steer him away, will you, Jennie? And pop in when you get the chance, I've got a bit of dictation.'

He returns to the minute, confident that, if the need arises and the unwanted visitor has nothing urgent to discuss, Jennie will use her considerable charm and diplomacy to keep the man out of his hair. The minutes pass and, as Don initials his handwritten minute, his secretary re-enters the office.

09.42 She seats herself, shorthand notebook at the ready. Being by

169

nature an inquisitive fly, you are curious to find out exactly how well the object of your attention conducts himself when it comes to dictation – and you don't have long to wait. Don, speaking in a regularly even voice, launches himself into the first memo.

'A memo, Jennie, to Mr Bromswold at Preston, copy to MD, Car Division, your ref CEB-stroke-LE-stroke-fifty-five . . . Thank you for your memo and enclosures of 10 August, stop. Brown has plainly had every chance to improve his conduct, comma, and I fully agree that this latest episode warrants the action you propose, stop. As you are doubtless aware, comma, his length of service is insufficient to qualify him in terms of any complaint of unfair dismissal, comma, and if your views remain unchanged, comma, I suggest you dismiss him forthwith, stop. I confirm that one week's pay in lieu of notice is entirely sufficient, stop . . . That's the first one, Jennie.'

Not at all bad, you think, a nicely modulated pace with no 'ums' and 'ahs' and a pretty good vocabulary, to boot. You listen with interest as Don proceeds with his next chunk of dictation.

'Another memo, this time to all on Circulation List 'B', reference as file . . .' He pauses and steals a glance at his watch. 'Look, I'll leave this one to you, Jennie. It's this hoary old business of apprentice awards – I expect you've read Joe's minute – we're still not getting the nominations in on time . . . Do one of your splendid reminders, will you?'

'Yes, certainly' Jennie replies, rising to her feet. 'You're due to see Tom Smithers at ten – and the union folder for your meeting at eleven o'clock is in your pending tray. Is there anything else?'

'No, I don't think so . . . I've just got time to sneak a look at my crib-notes on Tom . . . No, that's all, thank you, Jennie.'

As his secretary leaves, Don opens a drawer in his desk – and your proboscis quivers with anticipation as you watch him riffle through a number of small, 'penny notebook-type' booklets. He selects one with the initials 'T.S.' on the cover and swiftly scans the last scribbled entry.

Hum, almost a month since our last meeting . . . Tom should've sorted out the sales training at Gibson's by now . . . Ah, yes, and there's the revamped apprentice induction scheme – I must remember to quiz him on whether or not the colleges are playing ball. I'll bet there's some snag or other . . . Nothing else of note . . .

09.57 Replacing his crib in the drawer, Don resumes work on the journal proofs and is so engrossed when, a few minutes later, Jennie announces his first visitor of the day. Rising to his feet, Don welcomes the group's training officer and, after a brief exchange of pleasantries, indicates that they should settle themselves in a couple of easy chairs in the corner of the office. Within seconds, the two men are immersed in a wide-ranging and businesslike discussion. At one point, Jennie, entering the office in her customary unobtrusive fashion, without speaking, hands Don a note:

'Please ring Chief Exec a.s.a.p.'

Glancing briefly at the piece of paper and without interrupting the point he was making to Smithers, Don nods a quick thank-you to his secretary. Mentally biding his time, he waits for an opportune moment to arrive when he can do as he has been bid – and, a few minutes later, when Smithers is required to dig in his briefcase for some training data, he quietly excuses himself to make the necessary call. Luckily for Don, the chief executive's query, concerning the absence through sickness of one of the general managers, is swiftly resolved – and he is not obliged to apologize to Smithers for the distraction.

10.40 Their business concluded, Don ushers his visitor to the door – and while the two men say their goodbyes, you ponder on the conversation you've just overheard. There is no doubt in your fly's mind that while Smithers's efficiency of manner contributed much to the success of the discussion, there were several instances when Don, making good use of his flair for steering a conversation, contrived to keep the session nicely on track. Yes, well done, you mutter, as you watch him return to his desk.

Fishing out his personal crib on the training officer, Don, who is obviously not a man to trust things to memory, makes one or two notes for future reference. Then, replacing the booklet in the desk drawer and looking again at his watch, he rises abruptly from his seat and strides out of the office.

Slightly startled, you take to the air and buzz off in his wake.

Flashing a quick smile at Jennie as he passes her desk, Don moves purposefully through the open-plan area towards the corner where his redoubtable office supervisor, Sarah Farrell, has her position.

'G'morning, Sarah' he says affably. 'How are things – have you had any further trouble with the car?'

Laughing, she shakes her head. 'What, Mr Street, after the bill I've just paid – there'd better not be! No, seriously, it's going very well indeed, touch wood . . . Oh, by the way, I got McPhersons to give us a quote for the new index cards, and it's much better than the one from those Ironstone people. Look, here it is – what d'you think?'

Don examines the proffered estimate. 'Yes, you're quite right, it's some sixty quid less . . . Tell you what, get McPhersons to come up with some samples of similar work – and if they're okay, when the Ironstone rep comes in next week, we'll face him with them. Incidentally, Sarah, I'll want you in on that – after all, you're going to have much more to do with the new system than I ever will, so you must have a say in the final decision. He's coming some time next Tuesday morning, I can't remember the exact time – but check with Jennie, will you? Anything else before I dash?'

'No, there's nothing urgent – I've one or two points I'd like to discuss with you, but they can wait until this afternoon.'

Remembering in the nick of time that he has one of his regular staff 'hair-down sessions' scheduled for later in the day, Don nods. 'All right, I'll see you then. Try to get in ahead of the others, as arranged, and we'll have a quick natter, eh?'

Whoops, he's off again. Noting that Don is bound for the loo, you fly a few tactful circuits round the office while awaiting his reappearance. When finally he returns, you watch from ceiling height as he has a brief word with his secretary.

'Jennie, the shop stewards'll be here very shortly – wheel 'em in as soon as they arrive, will you? Right now, they'll all be having tea in the canteen – so you won't have to worry about rounding up something to drink.'

She nods gratefully. 'Oh, I'm afraid I've just put another

problem in your in-tray – there's a further development in the Harrison case.'

'That's all I need!' Don responds. 'Did you manage to dig out that stuff on the medical scheme?'

Jennie assumes a look of mock reproach. 'What the boss wants, the boss gets . . . It's all on your desk, sir.'

'Sorry, Jennie – and thank you! Well, once more, unto the breach . . .'

So saying, Don re-enters his office, to find that Jennie has already arranged five chairs in a semicircle facing the desk, thus setting the stage for the second appointment of his day.

With the wisdom granted to you as a know-all house-fly, you are aware that the meeting due to kick-off in a couple of minutes' time will not feature the cut-and-thrust tactics normally associated with management and union get-togethers. Surprisingly enough, this fourth in a series of regularly held, informal sessions with shop stewards will be entirely concerned with training feedback. One of the recent feathers in Don's cap was his success in persuading the group's management to allow certain trade union reps to attend a college-based, part-time TUC Shop Stewards' Course – and, as with the previous three sessions, this is what the meeting will be all about. Not unnaturally, the unions concerned were initially suspicious of Don's motives when he proposed that those attending the course should have an opportunity to discuss their progress – for, to them, it didn't seem anything like management's business to know what went on in a trade union activity. But, very much to his credit, he succeeded in convincing union and management alike that the proposal was wholly training-orientated – and certainly, thus far, his idea had met with success.

Of course, Don thanks his lucky stars that the group is happily unencumbered with hotbeds of union-management acrimony, and is well aware that the meetings would never have got off the ground had such conditions existed. As things are, he is convinced, if only in terms of improved communication, that both sides benefit from the occasional and informal natters.

11.01   Hearing the subdued hubbub as the shop stewards approach his office, Don replaces the small booklet marked 'TUC Course' in his desk drawer – confident that he has updated himself sufficiently well from his assiduously maintained crib-notes.

The door opens and, shepherded by Jennie, the five men file into the room – where, with some shuffling around and affable encouragement from Don, they finally get seated. Although by now accustomed to the meetings, the shop stewards still feel a definite unease on finding themselves in what, to them, is the plush domain of head office management – and Don is swift to sense their reaction. Commencing with a few words of light-hearted banter, mainly aimed at himself and couched in exactly the right terms to appeal to his audience, he wastes no time in getting the most extrovert member of the group to comment on the highlights of the latest course session. Within a space of minutes and due largely to Don's innate flair for steering a discussion, all the men are contributing in a lively and worthwhile fashion to the debate.

As the meeting progresses, your antennae pick up an occasional wave from the outer office, and you are pleased to note that Jennie, speaking with her customary blend of cordiality and polite firmness, is shielding Don from telephone calls and the odd casual visitor. Being wise in the ways of these humans, you are also gratified by the manner in which Don is refraining from making copious notes during the discussion, for you know that any such attempt might well inhibit the men from freely speaking their minds.

12.14　Sensing that things have been well and truly talked through, Don smoothly interjects his second and final summing-up into the flow of conversation – and, with a modicum of casual chit-chat, brings the meeting to a close. From the cheerful manner in which the men take their departure, it is obvious that they have derived benefit from the session, and you silently applaud your subject's efforts. Glancing at his wristwatch, Don stretches himself and restores order to the office. The second priority task in his schedule for the day has been successfully accomplished.

The chore over, Don asks Jennie to come in and sit down and reseats himself at his desk.

He gives a wry smile, 'Okay, then – what've you got for me?'

'No, you're all right!' Jennie replies. 'For once in a while, things have been fairly quiet! George Boon tried his luck once again, but I soon got rid of him – he'd like you to pop in to see him later today. It's nothing urgent – some query the pension trustees have raised about life certificates.' She consults her notepad. 'There were one or two phone calls . . . A Mr Paynton from the Department of Employment rang up for an appointment to discuss disabled employees – I've booked him in for next Thursday at eleven, and put a 'bring forward' on the file for you.' As she speaks, she makes the necessary entry in Don's desk diary. 'Ah, yes, and Eddie called – the doctor's cleared him to return to work, and he'll be back tomorrow morning . . . Now, if you like to sign these memos, I'll get them run off and into the mail before lunch.'

Don quickly scans the memos and appends his signature. 'Thanks, Jennie.'

'You've nothing on in the way of appointments for the rest of the day – except, of course, your 'hair-down session' at four o'clock. I'll remind them all about that later on . . . Is there anything else?'

'Oh, fine' Don responds, 'Let's see, I've got a bit more to do on the journal proofs, but, first, I'll take a look at this Harrison unfair dismissal business, and see what's to be done.' He pauses and casts a smilingly speculative look at his secretary. 'Hey, I think I've got a nice little job for you . . .'

'Oh-oh, I don't like the sound of that! What is it, Don?'

'D'you recall the memo this morning from the boss, clobbering me with the task of speaking at the Chamber of Commerce 'do' next month?' He picks the file and booklet on the group's medical scheme out of his pending tray and flourishes them at Jennie. 'Well, it's just occurred to me – how d'you feel about putting together some speaking notes for my big public occasion?'

'Goodness, I don't know . . .' Her eyes twinkle with sudden amusement. 'Putting words in the mouth of my boss . . .' She ponders for a second. 'Why, yes, I'd rather like to have a go!'

'What we need is a bare-bones skeleton for a spiel of, say, half an hour's duration – all about the difficulties we had in persuading the employees that there wasn't some kind of catch to the scheme. Tell you what, take a look at the folder for the last residential managers' course, there's some fairly typical speaking notes in amongst all the bumph.'

Don can tell by the look on Jennie's face that she is genuinely interested in the task.

'Right-oh!' she says briskly, rising to her feet. 'Who knows, if you like the result, I may even offer to write Maggie's next one for her . . .'

He guffaws. 'God knows, you certainly couldn't do worse than whoever's got the job at present! Now, we've both got work to do . . .'

You settle down on your fly's hunkers as Don, now alone, reaches for the Harrison file. The room is wrapped in silence, but the personnel manager's thoughts come through to you loud and clear as he studies the various enclosures.

Yep, that's right – we've made our response to the guy's complaint. So what's this latest letter all about? Ah, the crafty beggar – he's asking for a detailed statement of the reasons why he got the bullet . . . Hey, I'll have to be careful with this one, it could be a really hot potato . . . Let's see, the problem boils down to providing an accurate statement – and ensuring at the same time that I don't contradict anything that's already been said. That means I must go through each and every enclosure with a fine tooth-comb. Er, so far, so good – but what about the tribunal hearing? Is there any way I could prejudice our chances there by dropping a clanger in the statement? No, I'm sure that aspect is okay – the whole episode's documented accurately and everything's on our side. Now, there're two choices . . . I can limit the statement to the bare legal minimum, which'd probably be asking for trouble – or I can go the whole hog. That might have the effect of persuading the so-and-so that his complaint's not worth a light! Hum . . .

Rather than trust in his powers of dictation, Don elects to hand-draft the all-important statement – and, stealing a glance at his watch, commences to do exactly that. He is interrupted in his work by Jennie's voice on the intercom.

'Don, I'm going to lunch now – is there anything you want?'

'No, I don't think so' he replies. 'See you later . . .'

The thought of lunch reminds Don that he's feeling a mite

peckish, but, anxious to have done with the Harrison statement, he perseveres with his draft. For once, the words come fairly easily to mind and when, after some twenty minutes have passed, he subjects the page and a half of closely spaced handwriting to a final scrutiny, he is more than satisfied with the result.

13.02 You continue to look on as Don, heaving a sigh of relief, tosses the file with its accompanying draft into his out-tray. Aha, you think, it's about time we both had a break – at long last, the man's considering lunch ... As usual, your automatic interception of Don's thought-waves is spot-on. Grabbing a newspaper and rising from his desk, he crosses over to the corner by the door, where the hat-stand is positioned not far from where you squat. Tragically, his approach causes you to give an involuntary buzz – and, suddenly alerted to your presence, with one mighty swipe of the newspaper, Don squashes you flat ...

Yes, that's right, I lied in my teeth. If you happen to be an insect lover, it's not a happy ending – and, despite all my lofty squit at the beginning of this chapter, we both know that I've used it as a vehicle for a kind of summing-up. However, I do have a plea in mitigation of my skulduggery: quite simply, that it's been necessary – if only for the reason that I wish to round things off by giving you yet another job of work to do.

Having read the account of Don Street's day at the office (at least, it would've been a day had he not so abruptly terminated your existence), think about it – and then cast your eye over the following points. Most of them are pretty obvious – but, be honest, how many actually came to mind? And, even more important, how many do *you* put into regular practice?

- The *judicious* use of affable greetings and small-talk on arrival at the office.

- The private 'hair-down session' at the start of the day, primarily for the purpose of auditing one's progress and mentally sorting the hiccups. Yes, the mind will stray, but a regular and time-conscious application will soon work wonders in terms of objective thought – and that's what it's all about.

- Efficient use of the ubiquitous desk diary. The manager who makes a sustained and determined effort to formally allot priorities to his various tasks, and schedule times for their completion, is *not* a nit-picking pen-pusher – he is someone who has his feet firmly set on the road to efficient self-management.

- If he is wise, the manager who wishes to do more in less time will also ensure that his secretary is on the ball. Getting her into the habit, if necessary, of switching the telephone through to the inner sanctum when closeted with him is merely one illustration of a step in the right direction – provided, that is, *she* answers the thing if it happens to ring.

- A further illustration is giving her the freedom of your desk diary, and of making appointments on your behalf.

- One of the greatest deterrents to time-effective management is a poorly designed filing system. When did you last examine your set-up, and what did you do about it?

- And what about those minute sheets?

- But, of course, your office has a 'bring forward' system for files – or does it?

- Letters and other documents floating loosely around the office without the protection (and, so very often, the essential background) afforded by a file? How many unfiled papers land in your in-tray, and why should the morning mail be exempt from filing until after it's been inspected by His Nibs?

- Exactly how efficient is your secretary in guarding you against casual or unwanted visitors – and how diplomatically does she carry out this difficult chore? Maybe you don't allow her such autonomy of action – if not, why not?

- Ah, yes, the halitosis of management – bad dictation. Look, let's stop pussy-footing around – for the last time, if the cap fits, DO SOMETHING ABOUT IT.

- And, for goodness sake, if you have a secretary worthy of the title allow her to exercise *her* powers of composition. The odds are that she'll come up with better letters than the horrors you dictate. Or just perhaps, is that what bugs you?

- Circulation lists – It really is surprising how many otherwise efficient outfits overlook the use of standing circulation lists for internal correspondence. You know what I mean, a dirty great column of addressees at the head of a round-robin memo, instead of the simple words, Circulation List 'A', or what-have-you.

- How good is your secretary at automatically providing you with all that you need in the way of documents *prior* to a meeting, etc.? And would not a 'bring forward' system help?

- To all those managers who positively dislike putting pen to paper, the thought of Don's 'personal crib-notes' will be little short of anathema. However, to the executive who, caring for accuracy, is disinclined to place undue trust in memory, the maintenance of strictly private notes on selected people and topics may be of some appeal. If so, the ever-open desk diary is not the ideal repository for such confidential information – which is why Don, being an orderly guy, maintains his little collection of neatly labelled booklets.

- The account refers to our hero making good use of his flair for steering a conversation, and so it jolly well should. The ability to exert this *undetected* control over others is one of the vital keys to time-effective management.

- Do you recall the little episode concerning Sarah and the printing estimates? Don obviously had some reason for not delegating to his supervisor the whole task of meeting and dealing with the Ironstone rep – but he did insist that she was to participate in the final decision-making process. Which is as it should be.

- Regular staff 'hair-down sessions'? Enough said!

- Finally, you'll remember that Don's morning went on to include a spot of healthy delegation to his secretary (the speaking notes), and a clue that he was fairly well set on the path to effective problem-solving – to wit, his thoughts on the Harrison statement.

Way back at the beginning of the Don Street account, I referred to his possession of one sterling virtue, and suggested that you should be on the look out for it. In the main, this was a crude attempt on my part to get you to focus your attention on what followed, but I've had some second thoughts. Moving out to my accustomed position on the proverbial limb, I'm going to suggest that, albeit reading between the lines, Don's presentation conveys more than a mere impression of orderliness of mind – and that, reader, is a sterling virtue. If and when we happen to think about it (which is seldom), our very individual 'protection mechanism' prevents most of us from regarding our own mental processes as other than pretty damned good, especially when it comes down to such basics as orderliness of mind. The hard fact is that we are not nearly as good as we confidently assume, and the manager who prises away his own veneer by means of stiff and searching self-appraisal will find this out – and, I hope, will take energetic steps to bring about an improvement in his executive armoury. And that is very nearly that.

The old adage 'There are no bad Injuns, only bad Chiefs' contains more than a grain of truth, and well you know it. When you sally forth with your reinforced determination to squeeze the utmost benefit from those passing minutes, bear it in mind – and here's wishing you much power to your management elbow!

Recommended reading list

Specifically on the effective management of time

How to Use Your Time to Get things Done, Edwin B. Feldman, Frederick Fell, New York (1968)

The Time Trap, R. Alec Mackenzie, McGraw-Hill, New York (1972)

On timely communication

Effective Speaking and Presentation for the Company Executive, Clive T. Goodworth, Business Books (1980)

Janner's Complete Letterwriter, Greville Janner, Business Books (1983)

Plain Words, Sir Ernest Gowers, HMSO, London (1948)

On the timely conduct of meetings

ABC of Chairmanship, Lord Citrine, NCLC Publishing Society Ltd, London (1952)

Index

Activities at work
  'people', 59
  routine, 58
Air, travelling by, 154
Allocation of time, managers', 82
Alternative solutions to problems, 109
Attitudes, managers'
  to correspondence, 168
  to delegation, 81

Causes of problems, pinpointing, 108
'Cheating' when thinking, 99
Checking the outcome in problem-solving, 110
Commanding, the function of, 50
Commands, issuing, 83
Communication, secretary's skills in, 125
Component parts of an order, 84
Comprehension in thinking, use of, 95
Controlling, the function of, 50
Co-ordinating, the function of, 50
Correspondence, managers' attitudes to, 68
Costing work, 35, 37
Counselling, techniques of, 85

Dealing with paperwork, 72

Delegation, managers' attitudes to, 81
Diary, keeping a, 130
Dictation, managers' skills at, 76
Discipline, self-, 43
Duties at work
  'people', 59
  routine, 58, 67

Education/experience in thinking, factors of, 94
Employment legislation, 125
Employment life room, 14
Establishing facts in problem-solving, 107
Experience/education in thinking, factors of, 94
Explosion, the information, 74

Facts in problem-solving, establishing, 107
File minutes, 157, 168
File, useful types of, 167
Forecasting and planning, function of, 50
Functions of management, 50

Giving instructions, 83
'Grasshopping' when thinking, 61
'Gut feelings' when thinking, 94

Human relations, a reminder, 125

Impatience, managerial, 62
Information explosion, 74
Instinct when thinking, resort to, 94
Instructions, issuing, 83
Interruptions at work, 98, 116, 141
Issuing instructions, 83

Keeping a diary, 130

Lack of self-confidence, managers', 98
Laziness
  in general, 61
  in thinking, factor of, 99
Legislation, employment, 125
Leisure
  in general, 14
  at work, 28
Letters, dealing with, 68
Life room
  in general, 13
  work aspects, 14
List of examples
  time-wasters, 142
  work priorities, 136

Management
  functions of, 50
  solitude in, 98
Managers' time, allocation of, 82
Meetings, tactics at, 86, 141
Methodical outlook, developing a, 43, 46
Methods, reviewing, 97
Minutes, file, 157, 168

Obligations, work-related, 28
Order, component parts of an, 84
Organizing and timing work, 43, 47, 79
Organizing, function of, 50
Outlook, developing a methodical, 43, 46

Paperwork, dealing with, 72
'People' activities at work, 59
Planning and forecasting, 50, 97
Planning work for travelling time, 156
Pleas to staff, 84
Priorities, work, 36, 136
Problems, recognition of, 107
Problem-solving
  alternative solutions, 109
  checking the outcome, 110
  choosing the best alternative solution, 109
  establishing the facts, 107
  in general, 59, 105
  pinpointing the cause, 108
  six steps in, 107

Recognition of problems, 107
Relaxation at work, 122
Requests to staff, 83
Reviewing methods, 97
Routine activities and duties at work, 58, 67

Schedule, work, 132, 139
Scheduling work, 142
Secretarial skills, 123
Self-audit of work, 145
Self-confidence, lack of, 98
Self-delusion when thinking, 99
Self-discipline, 43

Shorthand speeds, secretarial,
124
Sickness, travel, 159
Six steps in problem-solving,
107
Skills at dictation, managers',
76
Solitude in management, 98
Speeds
shorthand, secretarial, 124
typing, secretarial, 124
Suggestions to staff, 83

Tactics at meetings, 86, 141
Techniques of counselling, 85
Telephone, use of the, 117
Thinking
'cheating', 99
comprehension, 95
'gut feelings', 93
in general, 59, 93
instinct, 93
interruptions to, 98
lack of self-confidence, 98
laziness in, 99
self-delusion in, 99
solitude in, 98
Time, allocation of managers',
82

Time-wasters
in general, 140
list of examples, 142
Timing and organizing effort,
79
'Tomorrow syndrome', 63
Travelling
by air, 154
by train, 154
work-kit, 153
Travel sickness, 159
Typing speeds, secretarial, 124

Use of the telephone, 117

Wasters, list of time-, 140
Work
costing, 35, 37
hours at work, 121
in general, 13
leisure at, 28
priorities, 36, 136
schedule, 132, 139, 143
scheduling, 142
self-audit of, 145
time spent in, 28
while travelling, 149
Work-kit, travelling, 153
Work-related obligations, 28